ACCESS ALL AREAS

ALSO BY SCOTT IAN

I'm the Man: The Story of that Guy from Anthrax
(with Jon Wiederhorn)

ACCESS ALL AREAS

STORIES FROM
A HARD ROCK LIFE

SCOTT IAN

Da Capo Press

Da Capo Press
Hachette Book Group
1290 Avenue of the Americas, New York, NY 10104
www.dacapopress.com
@DaCapoPress; @DaCapoPR

Printed in the United States of America

First Edition: November 2017

Published by Da Capo Press, an imprint of Perseus Books, LLC,
a subsidiary of Hachette Book Group, Inc.

The publisher is not responsible for websites (or their content)
that are not owned by the publisher.

Editorial production by Christine Marra, *Marra*thon Production Services.
www.marrathoneditorial.org

Book design by Jane Raese
Set in 9-point Parable

Library of Congress Cataloging-in-Publication Data has been applied for.

ISBN 978-0-306-82523-1 (hardcover), ISBN 978-0-306-82524-8 (ebook)

LSC-C

10 9 8 7 6 5 4 3 2 1

FOR PEARL AND REVEL,

I've been waiting my whole life for who came home today
You came in shining all this light so I could find my way
Now I can't wait to live this life you give
I'm not afraid.

Thank you for this beautiful lyric, Pearl.
It mirrors my heart.
You are my life, my love, my family.

CONTENTS

Bald of Confusion   1

Meet Me Under Ace Frehley   9

Fruit Loops   29

What If We Were the Dicks?   34

Everybody Hurts: NYC Suite, Part One   38

Sorry Never Felt So Good: NYC Suite, Part Two   43

Married with Children   50

The Wrath of Kirk   55

A Lesson in ~~Violence~~ English   65

All-In: Part One   70

The Land of Rape & S.O.D.   95

Beware the Leshy   104

The Most Boring Tour Story   113

Tsunami   115

Madonna   119

We Gave the Sun the Finger   132

The Walking Dead: My Life as a Zombie   140

That's Not a Rock   166

All-In: Part Two   170

The Conversation   198

Bathtub Pike   228

In the End . . .   231

Your Hero Should Never Wear Daisy Dukes   235

Acknowledgments   243

BALD OF CONFUSION

Hi, my name is Scott, and I play in a band called Anthrax.

I know you know who I am. You wouldn't be reading this book right now if you didn't. I just don't like to assume that you do because I feel like that would be kind of a dick move and lame to just assume that people know who I am. Like when people come up to me and say, "Hi, my name is _____ and I am a really big fan," and then when we shake hands I always say my name as well. If I was to just stand there staring back at them with a jerk attitude thinking, *Why yes, of course, you are a big fan and know who I am, and I'm not even going to recognize you as a human being by introducing myself,* that would be really shitty. Imagine if I were walking down the street and happened to see Angus Young and said, "Oh my God, it's Angus Young! It's really nice to meet you. I fucking love you and AC/DC so much! My name is Scott—how are you?" And he just said, "Uh-huh" like I'm supposed to know who he is. I'd be thinking, "I love you, Angus Young, but you're kind of a dick."

For the record, I've never met Angus. He's my hero, and he could probably put a cigarette out on my arm and I'd still pee my pants meeting him.

So I don't assume. I don't expect that everybody knows who I am, even though I have to say I know I have a recognizable head.

Bald. Heavy browed. Very beardy.

Recognizable.

And apparently very confusing.

I get it. I've been on TV. You may have been flipping channels late one night and glimpsed my face as you passed VH1 and it made an impression. And then you see me somewhere in public and are thinking, *It's that guy from that thing—I know him from somewhere. I KNOW HIM.* I know exactly when these thoughts are running through someone's brain. I can see it on their faces, the look people get when they are obviously not an Anthrax fan but just know my non-hipster-bearded-head from somewhere and can't quite put their finger on it and get really excited and come up to me and usually say something like, "Hey, uhh, I know you. You're famous—where do I know you from?"

My general answer to that is, "I don't know, sorry" because I really don't know who they think I am, and it's really not my responsibility to engage and educate the public at large. If they persist, I'll tell them I'm in a band called Anthrax. Sometimes that confuses them even more because they only remember seeing me as a talking head on some TV program and have no idea about the band. I'm very polite, mind you. I can only hope someone may be curious about Anthrax and go home and check it out.

Sometimes the recognition is stronger, and the person will know I am in a band (actual conversation):

DUDE IN THE AIRPORT: Hey, hey, HEY! [Actually yelling at me and then grabbing my shoulder to get my attention] You're that guy in that band! You're in a band, right?

ME: [A tiny bit annoyed at being grabbed waiting in line for coffee] I am.

DUDE IN THE AIRPORT: Which band?

ME: I'm in Anthrax.

DUDE IN THE AIRPORT: Nope . . . that's not it.

I'm not really sure how to answer that so I don't. It's not like I have a business card to prove it: *Scott Ian—Anthrax.* And this never happens in a record store where I could go grab a record out of the racks and show them.

Then there are the people who I think are actually fans, just very confused. I've had *so many* people ask me over the years, "Aren't you the singer of Anthrax?"

This is so confusing to me. I look nothing like Joey Belladonna.

And, "Aren't you the bass player of Anthrax?"

I look nothing like Frank Bello. Those guys have flowing locks of luxurious hair, and I have a stubbly egg for a head so, no, I'm neither of those guys, and I don't take the time to explain all of that and what I actually do in the band. Remember, these *conversations* are usually happening when I'm catching a flight or eating dinner with my family and it's neither the time nor the place.

I know a lot of these people who have made those mistakes have probably gone home and grabbed an Anthrax record, looked at the picture on the album, and said, "He couldn't just tell me he was the rhythm guitar player? What a dick!"

No, I couldn't tell you. It's not my responsibility. And maybe don't interrupt my conversation with my son about who would win in a fight between Batman and Darth Vader. Oh and also, I would never walk up to Steve Harris (if I need to explain who he is, you'd better put this book down right now, back away slowly, go home, and rethink your life choices) and say, "Aren't you the lead guitar player in Iron Maiden?"

It's not just that I get mistaken for guys in my own band either.

Back in the early 2000s there was a band from Los Angeles who got really big, and seemingly every time I got in a taxi the driver would look at me in his rearview mirror and do a stunned double take and yell, "System of a Down!" To this I would reply, "Yes! I am them!"

System of a Down are made up of four Armenians, and I guess there were a lot of Armenian taxi drivers in Hollywood in the early 2000s. At least this case of mistaken identity made sense because System's bass player, Shavo, was bald and also had an abnormal beard, so I understood. I would always go with this one because who am I to bum out the nice taxi driver? Who am I? I'm the prick, remember? I could act like a total jerk, and Shavo would get the blame. And then I see Shavo and he tells me, "You know how many times people come up to me and ask me if I'm Scott Ian?"

"Oh, really?" I mischievously answered. And then Shavo says, "Yeah, and then I act like a dick, and they get pissed at you."

Shavo wins.

All of this pales in comparison to a story my father-in-law told me. I also don't assume everyone knows that my father-in-law is Meat Loaf, so if you didn't know, now you do. He told me that he was sitting in his seat on a plane, and the woman sitting next to him asked, "Excuse me, sir—are you Jim Morrison?" This didn't happen in 1968; this was in the 1990s. Meat stared at this lady and finally said to her, "Yes. Yes, I am. I am Jim Morrison."

That's why Meat Loaf is my hero.

This whole confusion bit doesn't bother me all that much. Maybe it seems like I am crabby about it, but really it's pretty funny. Being someone who people recognize walking down the street because of my band is odd and cool at the same time. And now you, dear reader, know not to call me the hurdy-gurdy player in Arcade Fire.

There is something that I love about being famous, and it only happens exclusively in the worlds of hard rock and heavy metal. When I am walking down the street and a fan will see me and yell my name or the name of my band as loud as they can, usually prefaced with or dissected by the word *fucking*. Example: "FUCKING ANTHRAX!" and "SCOTT FUCKING IAN!" You know what I'm talking about. Maybe you've done it. We've all yelled, "SLAYER!" at bloodcurdling volume at some point in our lives. I have and worse.

In 1986 Anthrax got to open for Black Sabbath. Our first-ever big arena shows, and we're opening for Black fucking Sabbath. It was the second night of the tour, and their tour manager came to our dressing room to tell us that after the show Tony Iommi wanted to say hello and thank us for being on the tour. I was out of my mind thinking, *He's gonna thank us? We should be kissing those magic metal creating hands of his for all eternity.* After the show we got escorted down to some meet-and-greet room, we hung out for a couple of minutes, and then in walked Tony Iommi. I can still feel the sense of amazement I had at that moment, that I was standing in the same room as the man, let alone being on tour with him. So he walks in, and the temperature drops about ten degrees because he's so cool. He looked like a giant to me—I guess gods usually do (and I am a tall Hobbit at best). With his perfect black hair and his evil mustache and beard, and he's wearing a long leather coat that goes all the way down to the floor—I mean literally, if you told me he was Satan, I would have believed you. He was just so fucking powerful when he walked in that room. Maybe it was just because, gee, he only invented heavy metal, so you know, he is a little bit important to my life. But yeah, Tony Iommi walks in the room and shakes our hands and is thanking us, and in my fucking head I'm going shithouse bonkers and screaming, *TONY IOMMI! TOE NEE I OWE MEEEEEE!!! HOLY FUCK!* I wanted to grab him by the lapels and shake him and yell, "DO YOU KNOW WHAT YOU MEAN TO ME MOTHERFUCKER?!"

Of course all that hysterical screaming was done with my inside voice. I kept it inside because even the idiot twenty-two-year-old that I was knew it wouldn't be cool to grab Satan's lapels. And he had a giant security guard who would have kicked my ass right out of the room as soon as I even raised my voice, and then I never would have had a conversation with this proper English gentleman who invented heavy metal.

If we would've been outside on the street and I happened to see Tony walking by, different story altogether. I never would've been able to hold it in. I will never lose that feeling. Don't you ever stop screaming.

You may think I'm being sarcastic, but I'm not. I get it because I'm a fan too. I truly love that visceral can't-help-yourself reaction of screaming out the name of something you love so much. That feeling you get deep in your gut when you're at a show of a band you'd kill for and you just can't help but scream, "IRON MAIDEN!" You just can't help it; it's a primal emotion and a truly cathartic experience when you're surrounded by thousands of like-minded people.

Now imagine what it's like to be on stage and have thousands of people losing their minds for your band. It's an energy unlike anything anywhere else on the planet, and I love it. I live for it.

Like I said, this only happens in the world of hard rock and metal. It's very specific. It's not the high-pitched siren of pop adoration. It doesn't work in jazz. Or maybe I am totally wrong and back in the 1950s it'd be totally normal to hear someone gutturally scream, "CHET FUCKING BAKER" as loud as they could when they saw him walking down 52nd Street in New York City.

On the opposite end of the spectrum in the context of all this, the total bummer of being recognized, the most annoying thing, the bane of my pseudo-notoriety is people touching my beard. Men, women—they feel this need to touch it. What the hell is up with that? My beard is not public domain, yet people feel they have the right to just get their hands right in it, without even asking. I don't do that to people. I've never once thought at the sight of a bearded man to walk up and get my fingers entwined in his facial hair. Gross. What if I just walked up to a woman on the street who had beautiful hair and started running my hands through it? I'd get my ass kicked and arrested, yet ladies, you think you get a free pass at my beard because you're a lady? Fuck off. Your hands are filthy too, and I don't want them anywhere near my face. The only exceptions to the rule are my wife and son, and even my son, as much as I love him, gets the brush sometimes because he can have some dirty little hands. Call me nutso, but personal space is important to me.

If you are a bearded gentleman reading this, I know you feel my pain.

Now, all of that being said, I know a couple of guys in bands who feel much differently about beard invasions. They actually like it.

Next time Slayer comes to your town maybe they will be doing a record-store signing appearance or some kind of meet-and-greet at their show. Now pay close attention to these instructions—it's very important you follow these to the letter so you don't fuck it up. Wait your turn in line, and when you get to the band to get your stuff signed, shake hands, take a picture, etc., etc., and then you make your move. NOT ON TOM. Did I say that loud enough? Do not grab Tom's beard. He does not like that shit, and he'll get really pissed off and yell at you. Tom has a really loud and scary voice. Do you want him screaming at you in front of the band and a whole line of people? I don't think so. It's Kerry you want to engage. Now I know what you're thinking: *Kerry? Are you crazy? That guy will kill me if I touch his beard.* No, he won't. He has a very tough exterior, but underneath he's a big ol' softie, so get your fingers right up in his beard and give Kerry a good chin scratching like you would a cute little kitty cat and watch him purr!*

---

*In the history of the written word no one has ever written this sentence. Ever. You know why? Because it's completely insane and ridiculous. It's a joke. Don't touch Kerry's beard. Don't even think about touching Kerry's beard. One more time in case you got distracted: *Do not ever touch Kerry's beard.*

Zakk Wylde with his All-Father Odin beard wins when it comes to beards. His beard is like a rope that they use to tie cruise ships to the dock. It's truly the king of beards, and why wouldn't he want to show it off? So if you ever have the chance to hang with Zakk, grab onto that bridge cable of a beard and yank it hard. He's a big guy, so you may even want to use two hands to pull on it so he feels it.*

By the way, this is top-secret, behind-the-scenes info that we'll keep just between us, okay? I wouldn't want this to get out there publicly and then everyone will be all over those guys even worse than they are now.

---

*If you touch Zakk's beard, he will hammer you into the fucking floor like a nail.

I am the jumpy rhythm guitar player for Anthrax! Photo by Leon Neal.

MEET ME UNDER
ACE FREHLEY

In New York City in the late seventies, if you told someone to meet you under Ace Frehley, they knew exactly what you were talking about. Hold on, let me clarify that: if the person you were giving those particular directions to were somewhere between twelve and sixteen years old, they definitely knew what you were talking about.

To a generation of kids raised on Kiss in the seventies, Ace Frehley became our designated meeting point, our landmark. Except instead of a sign with an – *i* – on it, we had a giant live picture of Ace in all his smoking-guitar glory on the wall on the side of the entrance to Penn Station in Manhattan. This totemic landmark was a source of pride for all of us Kiss fans. We were an army always on the defensive, constantly ridiculed for liking a "comic book band." Publicly subjected to the derision and sometimes violent mockery of the older kids who wore their Led Zeppelin and Pink Floyd T-shirts aggressively like Gestapo uniforms, with our Kiss T-shirts the yellow stars of the oppressed. Heavy metaphor, I know. But when you're fourteen and are walking down the hallway in high school wearing the Kiss T-shirt you saved up your allowance for a month to buy and you walk past a crew of seventeen-year-old dudes who would knock your books out from under your arm, grab you by your beloved shirt, spit "KISS SUCKS, FAGGOT!" in your face, and then push you down onto the floor, ripping your shirt as you fell, well, that was certainly a fascist fashion statement. I'd be on the floor gathering my things, doing my best to ignore their taunts and smiling, not letting them have the satisfaction of getting to me, and all the while I am imagining myself grabbing a baseball bat from the equipment locker in the gymnasium and cracking their heads, singing "God of Thunder" as I swung. "What are you smiling at, faggot?" Pink Floyd snarled at me, snapping me out of my violent fantasy. I boldly stared back at him, smiling, the Demon on my shoulder nodding his approval. "Fuck him," Led Zep said as they turned to walk away. Pink gave one of the books I hadn't picked up yet a kick down the hall.

I watched them clomp off in their untied work boots, looking for some other unsuspecting member of our troops to torture.

Fucking burnouts, I thought as I headed to my next class, knowing that someday those losers would be fans of the band I was going to start. That's what I was thinking as I sat down at my desk in history class. I didn't let the burnouts get to me because at the ripe old age of fourteen I had had an epiphany. I was already on a path from which I would never stray. A path that instilled me with a fearlessness from the certainty of knowing what I was going to do with my life.

I can identify the exact moment, the specific time and place when I had such a powerful life-changing experience that it would shape and focus the rest of my life. Yes, my life has been made up of a multitude of experiences whose cumulative effect make me into the man I am today. But the event that started it all, that put me on the path to begin with, that I could pinpoint was on December 14, 1977, at Madison Square Garden in New York City when I went to see Kiss. Everything crystallized. Like Bruce Banner getting hit with the gamma radiation that turned him into the Hulk, I was irradiated by Kiss on that fateful winter night and walked out of Madison Square Garden with an absolutely clear picture of what I was going to do with my life: I was going to be in a band.

I WAS INDOCTRINATED into Kisstianity two years earlier in late 1975, the first time I heard "Rock and Roll All Nite" on the radio. It hooked me the first time I heard it, not even knowing what band was playing it, because the DJ never said the band's name. I was constantly singing the song, it was on a loop in my brain, and I was begging my parents to take me to a record store to try to find out who sang that song. I had to have it.

One night, not long after that, my brother and I were watching TV and I was flipping through all seven channels we had back then and saw these four guys in makeup and costumes with instruments. I paused, curious about how this band looked. They were just standing there making faces, and I thought they looked goofy. I was about to change the channel when the host said, "And now to play their hit song 'Rock and Roll All Nite,' here's Kiss!" Holy crap! The song! Peter kicked into the drum intro, and I lost it. My brother and I were jumping around and singing along, not believing what we were seeing. They went from looking goofy to the best thing I had ever seen/heard in my life. I was an eleven-year-old aspiring guitar player and a super-nerd comic book collector, and Kiss embodied my two favorite things in the world together in a band. If the host had come back out after the performance and said they were actually superheroes playing guitars, I would've believed it, that's how blown away I was. I had to have that song. I HAD TO. I was like a junkie looking for a fix. I planned to go straight to the record store after school the next day to find that song.

School was interminable that day. It was an endless drone of incessantly boring information dulling my brain. Kiss was telling me I needed to party every day, and I was stuck in fun jail. The only thing that kept me from running screaming out of that building to the sanctuary of the record store was the constant conversation amongst those who had seen—all of us who had borne witness to the majesty of Kiss. We would not be silenced. No matter how many times a teacher would yell at us to stop our whispered conversations about our new heroes, we kept on, passing notes when we couldn't speak of the pictures we had drawn from memory of their logo and talisman-like makeup. In the lunchroom, climbing on tables, playing air guitar, and singing the song out loud, lunch ladies screaming at us to get down, dull brown gravy dripping off the serving spoons they were waving at us. I'm sure these scenarios were playing out all across America that day as my generation had found its voice, and it was wearing seven-inch platform boots.

Finally the bell rang to end the day, and bulky school books in hand, I ran out into the cold New York winter air. I ran past the bus stop where a line of people stood waiting for a bus to show up. Normally I would've been in that line, the warmth of a bus better than walking the almost mile home in the cold, but I couldn't stand the thought of standing there waiting for even a minute when I could be moving toward my goal. So I ran. I ran through the cramp that was like a hot poker in my side to the shopping center where the record store was in my sight. I was sweating against the frigid air as I ran down a row of stores, weaving between people and catching annoyed looks from less anxious shoppers. The bells on the door of the record store rang noisily as I slammed through it, wild-eyed and out of breath, my jacket hanging off my shoulders and still clutching my books, stopping dead in my tracks in front of a rack filled with nothing but Kiss *Alive!* I stood there mesmerized. There it was, right in front of me, waiting for me to come get it, like it had always been there. I gently took one off the rack, caressing the plastic wrap with my fingers as I stared and stared and stared at the cover. The four of them in action, the makeup, the costumes, the lights, the smoke, the Kiss logo, the candelabra!

It was the best album I had ever held in my life, and I hadn't even heard it yet. I just knew.

From somewhere far, far away I could hear the Bryan Ferry–T-shirt-wearing record-store guy asking me if I needed any help. I didn't answer—I couldn't. I just kept staring, turning the record over and looking at the back cover, the two guys holding up the Kiss banner and an arena full of people waiting for the band to appear. I wanted to be those guys. I wanted to be in that arena. I was lost in a Kiss reverie when suddenly the album was being pulled from my hands and I came out of my trance: "Are you going to buy that? Your sweaty hands are going to ruin it." It was the record-store guy, quite bothered by this nonresponsive, sweating, red-faced kid who had dropped his books all over the floor of the store. "Umm, sorry, yes, I want to buy it. How much is it?" I asked. This irked him even more, as there was a sticker on the plastic that clearly read, "ON SALE ONLY $5.99." I had ignored the sticker while I was in my Kiss-coma. He wordlessly pointed at the sticker and handed the album back to me. He walked away, and I started staring again, about to fall back into the album cover when I had a terrible realization. $5.99.

$5.99?

I had seven dollars in my pocket, having saved up some allowance money to buy my father a birthday present. How was I going to buy the album if I only had enough money to get my father a birthday present? I had to have the album, and I had to get my father a birthday present. I was agonizing over this decision—what could I do? It was a Sophie's Choice for an eleven-year-old. The record-store guy cleared his throat loudly, signaling it was time for me to shit or get off the pot. I was gripping the album tightly in my hands, looking for an answer in the grease-painted faces of my idols when a lightbulb turned on and I knew what I was going to do.

I would buy the Kiss album and give it to my father for his birthday. Brilliant! I'd give him Kiss *Alive!* and he'd give it back to me. Yeah, I know: it was a selfish plan, but I was getting my dad a gift, and it's the thought that counts, right?

I brought the album up to the register, where record-store guy was sitting and reading *Creem* magazine (with Kiss on the cover). I paid for it and then annoyed him even more when I asked him to gift wrap it. He looked at me like I had stepped in dog shit and tracked it all over the store, so I pointed at the sign next to the register that read, "Free gift wrap with every purchase!" He hate-wrapped the album and wordlessly shoved it in a bag, his mood in no way affecting mine. I was very happy with myself, smiling like an idiot as I walked out of the store telling the guy to "Have a nice day!"

I got home and put the album in my closet. I had to put it out of my sight, as it was taking every ounce of what little willpower an eleven-year-old possesses to not unwrap the vinyl and crank it. Like a rock-and-roll Tell-Tale Heart, the album called to me; my only reprieve from its kick-drum heartbeat was while I was at school. A few days before his birthday I dared to take the album out of the closet to make sure it was okay. It felt hot in my hands and was practically screaming at me to play it.

My dad's birthday finally arrived, and I was so excited about the present I had bought for myself—I mean for my dad.

I handed my dad the present. I stood there watching, practically licking my chops as he unwrapped it. He looked at the album, confused for a second, and then he smiled and said, "Hmm, Kiss *Alive!* How did you know I wanted this?" For a moment I thought he was serious and that he was going to keep the album. That wouldn't have been a problem except for the fact that my parents were divorced and we didn't live with my dad. I'd only have visitation rights with the album a few times a month! My dad noticed the look of panic on my face and, smiling at me, said, "Thank you for this. Why don't you listen to it for a while and tell me how it is?" He handed the album back to me, and I ran to the stereo to put it on. I carefully took the record out of the sleeve, trying not to be distracted by the photo booklet that came with the album. I put the record on the turntable and with surgical precision, lowered the needle onto the record and was greeted by a monstrous voice yelling, "You wanted the best! You got the best! The hottest band in the world . . . Kiss!!!!!" and then the opening chords to "Deuce" mainlined themselves straight into my cerebral cortex and I was hooked.

I became a Kiss fanatic. They were my religion, and I was a radical extremist. Every conversation I had was about Kiss, either preaching to the choir of my Kiss-minded friends or espousing their greatness to recruit new army members. Every inch of wall space in my room was covered with posters and pictures of Kiss meticulously cut out of rock magazines. I had every album, doubles of the albums that came with extra stuff like the photo booklet in *Alive!* and the stickers in *Rock and Roll Over* so I could keep one set in mint condition and put the other set on my walls or school notebook. I got the Kiss action figures (by Mego), and I had the lunchbox and the makeup sets and anything they could stencil their logo on.

Over the next two years Kiss became my number-one priority. More important than the New York Yankees (although when the Yankees won the World Series in 1977 that took precedence for a moment—more on that later), comics (until Kiss put out their own comic), and skateboarding (we'd skateboard to Kiss blasting from a boombox). Kiss was everywhere and everything to me. I had it all, except for actually seeing them live. I would go to the record store at least once a week and ask record-store guy if he knew when Kiss was coming in concert and when tickets would be on sale. Back then the record store was where we'd go to buy tickets; it had a Ticketron machine. He'd tap a couple of keys on the computer-like machine and invariably respond with a very bored, "Nope" with an accompanying eye roll. Undeterred, I kept up with my weekly inquisition as school slogged on through the black-and-white New York City winter, the frigid days dragging one into another. The only thing that made it tolerable was the daily lunchroom Kiss Army meetings. We'd all bring our current Kiss-covered copies of *Circus, Creem, Rock Scene,* and *Hit Parader* and go through them with a fine-toothed comb looking for info on Kiss tour dates. Someone in our troop would always have some rumor of a show, some information disseminated by a radio DJ, and we'd wind ourselves up only to be disappointed by record-store guy tapping those Ticketron keys and muttering, "Nope."

Winter colored up into spring and then school's out for summer and what a summer it was. Summer of 1977 in New York City was an eventful one, to say the least, with its two-day city-wide blackout in July and the capture of Son of Sam in August. On the personal front my brother Jason and I got to escape the heat of the city when we flew out to Los Angeles and stayed at our mother's friend's house in Laguna Beach for a few weeks. For two kids from Queens, Laguna Beach was literally paradise. Every day we'd have to make a really difficult decision about what we were going to do first: go to the beach or go to the skateboard park. It was the best summer of my life until our second-to-last day there when I broke my left arm skateboarding. Even with that unfortunate accident, it was still an incredible summer.

When I got home and had the cast put on my arm my mood quickly changed. I couldn't play any sports, especially skateboarding, and more importantly, I couldn't play guitar. This really bummed me out, as playing along to Kiss records was one of my favorite things to do. Losing my ability to do that because of skateboarding put my priorities in order. Guitar first, everything else second. And then school started. My golden summer seemed like a distant dream as I dragged my one-armed ass back into the *Groundhog Day* everyday schedule of school. Not being able to play guitar was a huge deal for me: it was an outlet, a way for me to vent, and without it I was having a hard time. I still had Kiss records, and my comics and the Yankees were on the verge of going all the way that year—it was all just a bit dulled for me with my ability to play guitar taken away. It was going to be a long six weeks in a cast.

Walking home from school on a dreary fall day when all the leaves had already turned from a blazing melee of color to the limp calm beige of death, I decided to stop into the record store to see if there were any new records out that would cheer me up. I walked in, and the door chimes caused record-store guy to look over to see who was coming in to annoy him. I really wasn't in any mood to deal with his jerk Patti Smith–T-shirt-wearing attitude, so I decided not to ask him about Kiss. I was looking at Cheap Trick's *In Color* record when record-store guy said, "Hey kid, c'mere." I looked up from Rick Nielsen's picture and record-store guy was waving me over. This was a new development in our usually one-sided relationship, so I walked over, curious to see what he had to show me. I got to the counter, and he waved me over behind the register to where the Ticketron machine was. Now I was really interested—I was behind the curtain. He punched a couple of keys and pointed to the screen for me to read:

KISS DECEMBER 14 1977 MADISON SQUARE GARDEN
ON SALE SATURDAY KISS DECEMBER 15 1977
MADISON SQUARE GARDEN ON SALE SATURDAY
KISS DECEMBER 16 1977 MADISON SQUARE GARDEN
ON SALE SATURDAY

I stood there holding my breath as I read it over and over calmly thinking it through step by step. It was *Monday*. Tickets would go on sale *Saturday*. I would be getting my allowance from my dad when he came to take me and my brother to see the Yankees play the Dodgers in the World Series *Tuesday* night (yeah, that little thing was happening as well—no big deal!). I would have enough money to buy tickets. I WOULD HAVE ENOUGH MONEY TO BUY TICKETS!!! My screaming inside voice was interrupted by my new hero, Record-Store Guy!, smiling at me and saying, "The one day you didn't ask about Kiss tickets, and there they are." I was freaking out. Kiss was coming to Madison Square Garden, and I could buy a ticket! I had to get home and call my friends. "What time do they go on sale?" I asked as I was running out the door, and he said, "Hold on, there's something else—be right back." He walked to the back of the store and into the back room where they kept the stock. I was so antsy to get out of there that I was practically hopping from foot to foot ready to bolt so I could get home and call everyone and tell them not to spend any money because they'd need it for Kiss tickets, and then he walked out of the back room holding a poster. He handed it to me, and I unrolled it and screamed, "HOLY FUCKING SHIT!"

"It's yours, kid. Take it. They sent us a bunch. Now get out of here. You look like you're going to pee your pants," laughed Record-Store Guy! I was still hopping back and forth. My brain had exploded upon seeing the poster, and for a few seconds all I can remember were the sounds of crazed voices screaming, lunatic ravings in my head that sounded like the cat lady on *The Simpsons* crossed with the Tasmanian Devil, and then my brain slowly pieced itself back together and I realized it was just me standing there freaking the fuck out from a Kiss overdose. A concert *and* a new album? It was too much to bear. I checked to see if I had peed my pants because I thought Record-Store Guy! had said I did. Relieved that I had just misheard him, I calmed myself down as best I could, wiped the drool from my chin, and asked him again what time tickets went on sale. "Ten o'clock on the dot man. Don't be late."

I wasn't going to be late.

I got home and hung my new poster in my room. I told Jason about the concert, and he had money for a ticket. One less thing to worry about. Then I called my friends and told them about the concert and the new Kiss album. Everyone was as excited as I was; there was a lot of screaming down the phone lines. Now I just needed to convince my mom that it was okay for me and my brother to go without parental supervision—this was going to be just the guys. I started coming up with plans B, C, D, etc., etc., in case she said no. I made sure all my chores were done, and when she got home from work that evening I brought it up straight away. I told her that Kiss tickets were going on sale and that we had money to buy them (she knew how bad we wanted to see them) and that we were going to go with my friends. No chaperones. She was totally cool with it. "You're going to be fourteen. It's okay with me if you take the train in with your friends. Make sure it's okay with your father, and don't let your brother out of your sight. And you come home straight after the concert, okay? It's a school night." Shocked that that conversation went so easily, I thanked and hugged and kissed her and ran to my room to listen to *Alive!* I put on my headphones, laid down on my bed, stared at my new poster, and imagined being in the audience as the record massaged my brain through the Sennheisers.

I woke up the next morning in full-on Kiss Army mission-planning mode. It was Tuesday. First piece of business was seeing our dad that night and asking him for permission. Second was going straight to the record store after school on Friday to buy Kiss *Alive II.* I'd have enough money with what I had left from my previous two weeks' allowance and that current week's allowance to buy the record and a ticket. There was no way I could wait for Saturday morning knowing the new record was already in the store. And what if it sold out? Some of my friends were going with me to do that on Friday. Third, we made plans to meet Saturday morning at 7 a.m. at the record store so we'd be first in line. Fourth, we checked out the Long Island railroad schedules for December. Everything was coming together.

That afternoon our dad picked us up, and we went to Yankee Stadium for Game One of the 1977 World Series. I actually left my Kiss bubble that night. I'd been a Yankee fan longer than I'd been a Kiss fan, and for the moment my priorities changed. If the game had been on the same night as the concert, well, then, I would've had a huge problem. That would have been a conundrum that my young brain could not have solved, probably ending up with me having a stroke at thirteen. I didn't have to worry about making that decision, although I almost had a stroke when the Dodgers tied the game 3–3 in the ninth, forcing the game into extra innings. The Yankees finally pulled it out in the bottom of the twelfth inning, Willie Randolph scoring on a Paul Blair single, and the Yankees won 4–3, going one up on the Dodgers in the best-of-seven series. The game was unbelievably exciting and it was only on the way home I remembered to ask him if it was okay for us to go to the Kiss concert. He was totally fine with us going to the show sans adults, and he even threw in some extra cash with our allowances so we could get T-shirts and snacks. Things were really coming together better than I could imagine, and if that wasn't cool enough, we were going to Game Six of the World Series the following week.

THE NEXT TWO days flew by on a Yankee's win and new Kiss album/concert tickets high. On the way to school Friday morning I thought about skipping school or cutting my first few classes so I could go to the record store when it opened and get *Alive II* early. I thought that through and decided it was definitely not worth getting caught and possibly getting punished—no Kiss concert for you, young man. I was so high on Kiss and the Yankees that school wasn't even a buzzkill. When the bell rang to go home I ran, just like I did two years earlier, and Record-Store Guy! had a copy of *Alive II* held behind the counter for me. I devoured the record over the weekend. The live versions of "God of Thunder" and "Detroit Rock City" were my favorites on the record, and I liked the new original song "Rocket Ride" written by Ace, the best out of the four new tracks on side four. I listened to the record a few times back to back. And then around 11 p.m. I got into bed and set my alarm for six in the morning, even though I wasn't going to sleep—I was too excited about getting on line for tickets. I didn't think my mom would let me go to the record store right then and sleep over outside, so I squashed those thoughts and laid awake for hours stressing about the morning, worrying that there would be loads of people on line before us. I finally passed out at some point, and when I woke up I was sure I had slept through my alarm and missed getting tickets. It was 5 a.m. Cool. I got up, got dressed, and headed over to the record store, sure that there would already be people lining up. I was alone in the dark, sitting on the sidewalk in front of the record store until 7 a.m. when my friends showed up. I didn't care, by any means necessary. Now that it wasn't just me in line—well, there wasn't actually a line, just me and my friends—we could send someone to the bagel shop for bagels and coffee. Breakfast taken care of, we killed the time talking about *Alive II*. At 9 a.m. Record-Store Guy! showed up in a Kiss T-shirt and opened the store. He said, "C'mon in, diehards. Got a bagel for me?" We didn't want to get out of line in case anyone else showed up, but Record-Store Guy! said, "Don't worry, I know who's first." We browsed around in the store, and then around 9:30 a.m. people started showing up. I ran to the front register and stood there in case anyone tried to cut. By 10 a.m. there were people lined up all the way down the row of stores that the record store was on. I was standing at the register and got the first six tickets he printed out as soon as the Ticketron machine would let him. There was a seating chart for the Garden, and we had floor seats toward the back of the arena. We were fucking stoked, running home like Charlie Bucket, golden ticket in hand.

Over the next two months I would play *Alive!* and *Alive II* back to back, creating an epic Kiss concert in my room for me and my brother to air guitar and head-bang to in preparation for the big night looming ever closer. There was just the small matter of the Yankees returning home for Game Six of the World Series to finish up, and then I wouldn't have any other distractions from practicing Kisstianity. The Yankees were up 3–2 in the series and only needed to win Game Six to be world champions, and win they did, in dramatic fashion. Reggie Jackson hit three home runs, and the Yankees won their first World Series since 1962. Being a part of that victory at Yankee Stadium was an unbelievable moment, the absolute high point of my life, and I rode that October Yankee win all the way to Madison Square Garden where I would go even higher.

DECEMBER 14. K-DAY FOR ME and my friends. At school that day everyone was buzzing about the concert; seemingly the whole school was going. We actually had tickets to the first of three sold-out shows. Mine was safely tucked in my wallet, having already checked on it a dozen times that day. The plan was to go home after school, drop books, get some pizza at Jack's Pizza in the shopping center across from where we all lived, and then take the bus up to the Long Island Railroad station where we would take the first train we could to Penn Station in Manhattan, which was right underneath Madison Square Garden. We wanted to get there as soon as we could so we would have more time to hang out at the Garden and be a part of it all. This was a big fucking deal for us. Six of us kids in the city to see Kiss with no parents. We'd made it!

The cold and windy train platform heading to Manhattan was crowded with people going to the show. It was a scene: teenage girls in hot pants and heels, hair feathered and eyes shadowed, leather jackets zippered tight around their bodies against the cold, smoking their Marlboros. Long-haired bell-bottom-wearing dudes in their green Army-Navy store military jackets, drinking Bud from brown paper bags. And there was us, three thirteen-year-olds, two twelves, and my ten-year-old brother hanging on the periphery, allowed to coexist in that moment with the teenagers. We'd even got a few head nods from some of the guys and offers of beer and cigarettes and even the opportunity to buy weed. We gladly took a couple of beers, none of us smoked cigarettes, and we didn't have money to buy weed—all our cash was earmarked for Kiss swag.

We were enjoying our moment of acceptance by the older kids. The common denominator was that everyone was wearing a Kiss T-shirt. If this had been a normal day, someone would've already thrown an empty beer can at us and told us to fuck off, so we shared the three beers between us, none for my brother, and did our best to look cool. I had no intention of getting fucked up and ruining my night.

When the train pulled in, the cars were already crowded with people going to the show. Add in everyone who got on the train at Bayside station, and it was packed. We stood right by the doors, pressed against each other, struggling to even be able to raise a beer up to our mouths in the crush. The train car quickly filled with the smell of pot as we hurtled toward Manhattan, wide eyed and excited to be a part of this world we had only imagined. I felt right at home. When we got to Penn Station we hurried off the train to beat the crowd and ran up the steps from the platform and into the teeming madness of the station. There were thousands of people heading every which way, commuters trying to get home from work and, of course, all of us Kiss fans. The six of us made our way to a less crowded area of the station to figure out what we were going to do. We were very early—the show wasn't starting for another two hours—so we needed to do something to kill the time. While we were standing around figuring that out, a guy carrying a big duffel bag came walking up to us, pulled a couple of shirts out of it, and said, "Youse guys wanna buy shirts? I got 'em cheapuh here than they are inside!" He was holding up a Kiss T-shirt that had the *Love Gun* album cover on it, and it looked pretty good. My brother and I decided we were going to wait until we got upstairs to the Garden to see what other options there were. My friend David bought one, and then my other friend Ronnie asked the guy if he had one in a large, and the guy said, "Yeah, yeah I do. I have to run over there"—he pointed off toward the crowds—"to where my udduh guy is and get one offa him. Gimme the ten bucks and I'll be right back." Ronnie looked at the guy and then he looked at all of us with a *What should I do?* look on his face. We all looked back with the same look, afraid to piss the guy off. The guy said, "Wha'dya think I'm gunna do? Take your money and run? C'mon, kid. I'm just trying to earn a buck here. You want the shirt or not? Your friend likes his." Ronnie pulled out his wallet and gave him the ten bucks, and the guy took off to get his shirt. Ronnie said, "He seems okay. He gave David his shirt, right?" I personally wouldn't have given the guy a dime without having the shirt in my hand first, but I tried to make Ronnie feel okay about his soon-to-be fuck-up: "I'm sure he's cool. Don't worry. He'll be right back," I said, my other friends looking at me incredulously. We waited five, ten, fifteen minutes, and the guy never came back. Ronnie got robbed for the money he had for a shirt, and he was crying and saying he wanted to go home. We couldn't let him leave by himself—our parents would kill us—and none of us were going to leave and take the train back to Bayside. We all decided we would chip in a couple of dollars each so Ronnie could get a shirt too. And we'd share whatever food and drinks we bought with him. Ronnie stopped crying and thanked us and said he was sorry for fucking up.

Ronnie getting ripped off was our cue to get out of the train station. We rode the wave of Kiss fans up the escalators and out of Penn Station onto 7th Avenue. We were immediately accosted by half a dozen guys selling shirts with every different Kiss album cover. They were practically shoving them in our faces. I bought a shirt with the *Destroyer* album cover on it and a big gold-colored Kiss logo. My brother and the rest of the guys all got shirts too. Shirts in hand, we made our way through the crowds and into the entrance to the Garden. Doors were open, and we figured we would go find our seats and get out of the insanity for a few minutes. I stopped at the merchandise stand and bought the *Alive II* tour program and then we headed to our seats. The inside of the arena wasn't nearly as crowded as the train station or outside on 7th Avenue. Most of the people were outside partying, which was fine with me. I was happy to sit there for a minute and look at the pictures in the tour program. I was just settling in to do that when the lights turned off and a band started to play. I looked at my friends: "Who the hell is this?" I yelled over the band. Nobody knew what was going on. I had no idea there was a band on before Kiss. I didn't want to see any other band, and apparently neither did anyone else already in the arena because between songs the crowd would chant, "Fuck this! We want Kiss! Fuck this! We want Kiss!" We all chimed in as well, although the band was actually pretty good. Turns out they were a band called Detective fronted by Michael Des Barres, and I bought their record the week after the show. Detective did their job, because I was all riled up from chanting to get them to stop playing, and now they were done and I was only minutes away from the definitive moment of my life.

The lights went out and the roar from the crowd was deafening. I was standing on my seat so I could see the stage over the sea of people in front of me. And then that giant voice from Kiss *Alive!* was booming all over the arena: "NEW YORK CITY!!!" And the crowd roared back its approval at hearing the name of the city where they lived. "YOU WANTED THE BEST! YOU GOT THE BEST! THE HOTTEST BAND IN THE WORLD—KISS!!!"

I was jumping up and down on my seat, hands in the air like I was riding a roller coaster, and then I saw them. I could see them on the stage: Peter behind his kit, Ace walking out onto stage left, Paul playing his guitar in the center, and Gene stalking stage right. I was in the same room as Kiss! I was screaming as loud as I could, in a complete frenzy. Paul was playing the intro to "I Stole Your

Love," but I couldn't even make out what he was playing in the moment because I couldn't hear it over my own screaming as well as the other eighteen thousand people doing the same thing. The band kicked in, and it wasn't until the chorus of the song that I could even understand what song they were playing. I had never heard anything so loud in my life. The combination of the volume of the crowd and the band was deafening to me, and it didn't matter one bit. After a minute my ears adjusted to the volume, like tuning in a radio station, and everything sounded loud and clear. From that point on I lost all sense of myself as I lost my mind, swept up into the mass consciousness of the crowd, all of us shouting it out loud as one. I'm not going to go into a song-by-song breakdown of the whole set—suffice it to say that they played all the hits and I sang every word to every song along with my brother and friends. Gene blew fire and spit blood. Ace's guitar smoked. Paul smashed his guitar. They had massive walls of amps with steps climbing to the top of them. They had the giant Kiss logo flashing behind them. At the end of their final encore song, "Black Diamond," Peter's drum kit rose high up above the stage along with the rest of the band standing on hydraulic platforms as concussion bombs went off, and we screamed and screamed and screamed for more. The lights came up, and eighteen thousand people had the same delirious look of sheer satisfaction on their faces. We had all climbed the mountain and were found worthy. The concert was the culmination of having fanatically worshipped at the altar of Kiss for two years. It was everything I wanted it to be and more. I was filled with energy, a burning light inside my brain, my heart pounding, the power of Kiss compelling me, showing me my path, and as I left Madison Square Garden that night I stepped foot onto that path and have walked it for the last thirty-nine years, three months, and two days. And I will never stray from it.

Kiss has been the one musical constant in my life since then. They've been my longest relationship. They're in my blood, literally: I have Gene Simmons tattooed on my leg.

If it weren't for Kiss, I wouldn't have started a band. I wouldn't be writing this book. My life would've taken a different path down who knows what unknown roads. It was Kiss who sent me on the righteous path of rock. Sure, I got into much heavier music, but it was Kiss who opened the door for it all.

Thanks, Kiss.

FRUIT LOOPS

I've done a lot of interviews over the last thirty-three years. A LOT. It's safe to say that the number is somewhere in the thousands, and of those thousands of interviews and tens of thousands of questions I've been asked there's one question I've been asked more than any other:

"What is the craziest thing you've seen on tour?"

A man running down the street full speed taking a shit.

No, I've never seen that. That's from a George Carlin bit about things you never see. My answer is crazier than that. You would sooner see the running dumper than the scene I am about to describe. It's a scene I have a hard time believing actually happened, but it did. I was there. I bore witness to a game—or, better yet, a contest—that I couldn't/wouldn't have ever imagined, and I have a big imagination. I can only surmise that the idea of setting up this scenario was to create something that had never been seen before, a scene so original (that's one word for it) that it may have never happened in the history of the world as far as I know. Or maybe it happened the night before on the tour I witnessed it on, or maybe it was happening every night backstage on that tour and it was all new to me. There are many questions I have about this event; they continue to pile up as the years pass. The main ones being: Who made the rules of the contest, and how did they get the participants to agree to take part?

And why Fruit Loops?

So what is the craziest thing you've seen on tour?

An enema contest.

Nine Inch Nails played Madison Square Garden in December of 1994 on their aptly named Self Destruct tour. Marilyn Manson and the Jim Rose Circus were the openers. The show was amazing, unlike any other rock show I had ever seen. Trent Reznor and his band played like they were on death row and their executions were the next day. The stage—at least from my point of view from the audience and as a fan and someone who does this for a living—looked like a physically dangerous place to be. It really seemed like they were working out some shit up there. It was a great show, and there's so much more to say about it, but I'm not here to review the show. I'm here to answer my most asked question.

After the show I went backstage with my friend Jennifer Syme. She knew the Manson guys and was able to get us passes. She introduced me to Brian and Jeordie, aka Manson and Twiggy. I was already a fan, and it was cool to find out they were Anthrax fans as well. Jeordie told me a story about how he was a stagehand at a show we played at the Cameo Theater in Miami in 1987 and how he stole the NYHC (New York hardcore) button off my guitar strap. I remembered immediately, as I was actually pissed off at my tech at the time because I thought he lost it! Jeordie! He told me he still had the button and would give it back to me. I told him he had to keep it—it was his now.

I was talking to some guys I knew on the local Garden crew backstage when Jennifer came over and whispered to me, "There's some weird shit about to go down in the Nine Inch Nails dressing room. Do you want to go check it out?"

I said good-bye to my friends, and Jennifer and I, always down for weird shit, headed over to the dressing room.

There was a security guy outside the door to the dressing room checking passes. Apparently you had to have a specific pass to get into the inner sanctum. We didn't have the right passes, but we had my laminate face. The security guy recognized me and was a fan, so one handshake later we were on the inside. It was a large room, crowded with people all anticipating what the postshow festivities were going to be. There was a large high-backed throne-like chair set up against a wall facing into the room, and sitting there was Trent Reznor, drink in hand, surrounded by a gaggle of people in all kinds of altered states of undress, physical and mental. It reminded me of Gary Oldman in *Bram Stoker's Dracula* surrounded by his sexy vampire minions. The king was holding court, and as if on cue, in walked his jester. Jim Rose came Joker-smiling into the room with three girls. Ever the ringmaster, Jim went into his patter, introducing everyone to these wonderfully adventurous ladies who were going to participate in an amazing contest for our collective enjoyment, all, of course, brought to us by and with the blessing of Trent. What kind of contest, you ask? With a glint in his eye and that mischievous smile on his lips, Jim told us, "Why, an enema contest. An enema contest, my good people!"

And then Jim regaled us with the details of what was about to happen. The three ever-so-game ladies were going to remove their pants and undergarments and get down on their hands and knees. Jim and his assistants were filling enema bags with beer, and then they would administer—"Oh, administer sounds so clinical, and we're all here to have fun tonight, especially our three beautiful girls partaking in this historic event" (Jim could talk). Jim and his assistants would help the three beautiful women enjoy their beer enemas, and then our three lovely ladies would do their best to hold the beer in as long as they could. Then Jim was placing what looked like cereal bowls underneath each girl so that when they couldn't hold the beer anymore they would let go into the bowls. Then Jim filled each bowl with Fruit Loops.

If I stopped here, it'd already be quite a tale. Don't say I didn't warn you. I wish someone would've said to me in that moment, "Hey, this is a weird scene. Let's get out of here." Would I have left? Hard to say. I was curious and drunk. The energy in the room was dark, uncomfortable, contagious, and building to a fever pitch. A sacrifice-the-virgins-at-the-altar kind of vibe. People wanted a show.

I remember thinking, *Why is he filling the bowls with Fruit Loops?* Jim would elucidate, "My friends, I'm sure you've noticed the bowls filled with a delicious breakfast cereal, Fruit Loops to be exact. Ahh the joys of youth! As each one of our enema angels releases, they will let go into the bowl below them. Then . . ." — dramatic pause—"our winning girl, the girl with the most secure sphincter, GETS TO eat the cereal!" Jim had a way of making the most disgusting, degrading thing I had ever heard almost sound fun.

And so it began. Jim and his guys gave the girls the enemas, and the girls did their job as best they could. A winner was crowned, and she had a bite or three of the delicious breakfast cereal after some cajoling by our master of ceremonies who was doing his best to keep everyone happy. It had turned into a tough room. Maybe it was just me projecting my feelings on everyone else, but the vibe had really gone negative, as it should have. And it smelled. The room smelled bad, like nervous armpit sweat and stale beer and ass. The initial excitement of being in that room, speculating what might happen, had just turned into a shitty juvenile gross-out fest being stared at by a bunch of leering pervs. At least that's what I felt like. The three girls weren't bummed out; in fact, they were all smiling as they got dressed and were handed drinks and being congratulated by people.

I bumped into Jim Rose on our way out, and he told me that it was his gig to set up some kind of scene backstage every night and that the enema thing was pretty standard. *Where do you go from there?* I thought.

Jennifer and I left the room and found a drink. We both felt like we needed a shower after what we had witnessed and just wanted to get drunk again and have fun.

Oh, by the way, I've been off Fruit Loops since.

WHAT IF WE WERE THE DICKS?

Late at night and Sunset Boulevard feels like Hopper's *Nighthawks* painting as Charlie Benante and I walk back to the Hyatt on Sunset—or the Riot House, as it was affectionately known—after a post-show meal at Mel's Diner. We were walking past the temple of 1980s stand-up, the Comedy Store, when I noticed a guy standing outside the main entrance having a smoke. I stopped dead in my tracks.

"Holy shit, it's him!" I whispered excitedly to Charlie as I sneakily pointed at the long-haired beret-wearing dude standing there.

"Jeez, it *is* him! Hahaha, holy shit—what should we do?!" Charlie quietly exclaimed back.

"Fuck it! Let's go say hello. We have to—it's Sam Kinison!"

SAM KINISON.

The man was a hero to us. He had reinvented stand-up comedy in the 1980s, and we knew every one of his bits by heart. We loved Sam so much that we had sampled his trademark scream in our song "I'm the Man" two years before this chance meeting. And unlike most thieving artists at the time, we actually sent our song with the sample in place to his management for approval, and they said we could use it and that Sam was a big fan of the band. So we had that going for us as we nervously walked up to this larger-than-life pirate of hilarity.

Sam saw us walking toward him, and before he could turn and escape back into the club I reached out to shake hands and nervously said, "Sam, hey, how are ya? I'm Scott and this is Charlie from Anthrax. We sampled your scream on our song, and we wanted to thank you." I could see a dim light bulb of recognition flicker in his eyes, so I repeated, "We sampled your scream in our song 'I'm The Man.' We're in the band Anthrax."

Then the dim light bulb turned into a flaming torch, and Sam was practically yelling, "Hey guys! Hey how are ya? Nice to meet you! Love you guys! It's so cool that you used me in your song! Hahahaha!" he cackled with that amazing laugh of his.

Charlie and I were really excited now, our hero remembered us. "What are you doing here?" I asked and then immediately kicked myself for asking such a stupid question. He's a comedian standing outside a comedy club. Duh.

Sam wasn't bothered though, and said, "I'm just getting ready to get out of here."

"Would you mind taking a picture with us really quick before you split?" I asked, figuring I wasn't stepping over any boundaries and he did say that he loved us.

Sam pointed to a car in the parking lot and quietly said, "Hey guys, ya see that convertible over there?"

"Yes," we replied.

And then Sam leaned in conspiratorially and asked, "And do you see that hot blonde sitting in the passenger seat?"

"Uh huh," we replied.

"Well, I'm going to get in that convertible, drive that hot blonde up to my house in the hills, and fuck the shit out of her. Then I'll drive back down here and take that picture. I promised her I would do this, so you guys just wait right here and I'll be right back."

Charlie and I looked at each other, not knowing if he was joking or what was going on, so I said, "Dude, that's cool. Hell yeah, but can we just snap a pic real quick and . . ."

"DO YOU SEE THAT CONVERTIBLE OVER THERE?!" Sam yelled, interrupting me. Suddenly he was pissed off, red in the face, and aggro, "AND DO YOU SEE THE HOT BLONDE SITTING IN IT?!" Charlie and I were frozen, not knowing what the fuck was happening. All we wanted was a quick picture with our hero, and now we're getting berated by this maniac. Cocaine is a hell of a drug.

Sam kept on it, spittle flying from his lips: "I'M GOING TO DRIVE HER UP TO MY HOUSE AND FUCK THE SHIT OUT OF HER! YOU GUYS WAIT HERE, AND I'LL DRIVE BACK DOWN AND TAKE THAT PICTURE! UNDERSTAND?" he said oh so sarcastically.

"Uh yeah, whatever dude," I muttered, but Sam wasn't paying attention. He was already heading toward the convertible and the rest of his night/morning/life with the "hot blonde." Charlie and I walked off, heads down, not believing what had just happened. It wouldn't have been so bad if he'd just told us he didn't want to take a picture, but to yell at us and tell us to wait for him in front of the Comedy Store at 3 a.m. like a couple of jerks while he fucked some slut? Dick move, Kinison. I was bummed, but fuck it—I still loved his comedy. So he was a dick. A really funny dick. And that was that, end of story. Good night, Los Angeles.

A FEW YEARS LATER I woke up to the terrible news that Sam Kinison had died in a car crash. It was so sad and tragic. He had quit booze and drugs, and after a couple of shitty years his career was on the upswing again. I could imagine him screaming, "I stop doing cocaine and I stop drinking booze and I give up the sluts and I get married and then I GET KILLED IN A FUCKING CAR CRASH AH AHHHHHHHHHHHH!!!" I put on his *Louder than Hell* record and laughed my ass off and thought back to that night when Charlie and I met him outside the Comedy Store and he wouldn't take a picture with us.

And a dim light bulb of an idea started to glow in my head: What if Sam had kept his promise that night and did come back after fucking the shit out of the hot blonde only to find me and Charlie gone? And that light bulb glowed brighter, and I wondered, what if he got back to the Comedy Store and had planned on hanging out with us, taking us for a ride in his convertible, and partying all night long Sam style with his heavy metal friends? To Sam, Charlie and I were rock stars, so why wouldn't we wait to hang out with him? We'd understand that he was just going to blow a load and then come right back to really have some fun with his bros! We had all night to hang—of course we would wait for him.

Sam didn't know that we didn't hang like that. His scene was definitely not our scene, so we split. Now the idea was burning in my brain: What if he got back and saw that we didn't wait for him and said, "Dick move, Anthrax."

What if we were the dicks?

AH AHHHHHHHHHHHHHH!!!

Illustration by Stephen Thompson.

EVERYBODY HURTS

NYC Suite, Part One

"Yo mosh, David Lee Roth is going to some party in Soho. It's going to be off the hook. Let's roll with him over there and check it out!" Dominick yelled.

"What did you say?" I yelled back, not hearing him over the din of indiscernible hip-hop and a hundred inane conversations. We were upstairs at Café Tabac, and on a blurry December night in 1992 we were at the epicenter of New York City nightlife fabulousness. Or douchiness, depending on how drunk you were.

Dominick DeLuca (who nicknamed me Mosh in the late 1980s) was my best friend, chosen family, and partner in crime. You may remember him from MTV's *Headbanger's Ball*.

Dominick and I were regulars at Tabac because we were friends with the door people, and that's like having the keys to the kingdom. Learning this secret to the sanctum-sanctorum's of New York City nightlife was the key to my Bukowskian lifestyle throughout the 1990s. We always had a table, but most importantly, we had free drinks.

"There's some Christmas party at a loft in Soho. It's supposed to be nuts. David Lee is heading over there with a bunch of people, and we can tag along!" Dominick exclaimed again louder this time so I could hear him over the Patrick Bateman look-alike who was yelling at the hostess because he wasn't getting a table and "If he WASN'T TAKEN CARE OF THIS FUCKING SECOND, she would be LOOKING FOR A NEW JOB TOMORROW!" I nodded toward the stairs, and as we were walking out we purposely hip-checked past American Psycho as he was madly gesticulating over the table we had just left.

Protected by a layer of vodka, we stumbled out of the steamy Café Tabac into that get-in-your-bones cold that New York City does so well and grabbed a cab to Soho. I was feeling no cold—or pain, for that matter—and was really excited to be heading to some random party that David Lee Roth was going to be attending.

I had met Dave in 1988 when Anthrax and his David Lee Roth band were on tour in Europe as part of the Monsters of Rock Festival with Iron Maiden. It was a great tour for many reasons, one of them being we were pretty much playing stadium shows on the weekends and would have the rest of the week off to travel around Europe and eat, drink, sightsee, and trash a bunch of Mercedes (read my book *I'm the Man* for that story). So I'm walking backstage at some stadium in Germany, and I see Dave sitting in a folding beach chair outside his dressing room trailer. Next to him there's a small tent pitched and the remnants of a campfire. Dave's reading a comic book. That was all the icebreaker I needed (I am also a comic book guy), so I walked over and introduced myself. We talked about comics and the tour for a bit, and then I asked him about the tent. He told me that because we had so many days off between shows, he decided to travel on his own and would get to the festival sites two days early and just camp out backstage until the festival "came to him." Of course this was all said in his inimitable Dave way, with his Cheshire cat grin practically lopping off the top part of his head. Over the next six weeks I'd see Dave, comic in hand, walking around backstage, and he always said hello. Cool dude.

The taxi pulls up to some nondescript old Soho warehouse building—this was 1992, and Soho then wasn't the Soho it would become just a few years later. It still had a bit of the Wild West, anything-goes vibe about it, and loft parties were always an adventure. Dom and I headed up the five stories to the top floor. We were both sucking air when we got to the loft and made a bee-line straight to the bar to regain the buzz we had lost on our un-wanted turn on the Stairmaster.

We quickly did shots to catch up and then filled some Solo cups with vodka and cranberry and shouldered our way through the mob looking for Dave and his crew. I had my head down, eyes la-ser focused on not spilling my drink as we made our way through the giant loft space on our quest. I figured maybe we had beaten him there or maybe he'd found somewhere better to go. He was David Lee Roth for fuck's sake. Wherever he is, IS the place to be.

Dom and I found a not-so-crowded spot to chill and drink our drinks. We made a "toast to the extras," as we used to say, because that's what going out in New York City felt like. Every night at some bar or club or loft filled with the same people having the same hubbub-hubbub conversations in the background like they were hired right out of Central Casting. I'd go home to Los An-geles for a few weeks and then come back to the city and go out and see the same people. A who's who of who's that, and everyone wants to hug you hello and shake your hand three ways like you're best friends.

As much as Dom and I went out, we were never scene fixtures, just filling up space, programmed to entertain.

For us it was all about stick and move.

There was some commotion over on the other side of the party, and we could see some of the people who were rolling with Dave. We walked over to see what was up, and there was Dave holding court, regaling anyone within earshot with some too-good-to-be-true-but-it's-Dave-so-they're-all-true anecdote. At some point I caught eyes with Dave and stepped in to say hello. I kind of knew the guy, so I figured I wouldn't be bugging him. Dave was all smiles as we shook hands and I said, "Hi Dave. Happy holidays!

It's been a while since we toured in Europe. Nice to see you!" Dave still had my hand and still had the smile frozen on his face when he said, "Nice to meet you man. Happy holidays to you as well!"

Nice to meet me? I was confused because we had met and hung out a bunch on that tour a few years earlier. Dave had already focused his smile elsewhere as I stood there already over the fact that Dave had no idea we had met before. I was just happy to be standing in his orbit, drinking my drink and stupidly musing on what it would be like to be David Lee Roth.

Our drinks now happily swimming in our bellies, we headed back to the bar for more. We figured we'd do a shot and then find somewhere else to blag free booze. Dom had already heard about some other party, so we made our way back to the bar and had two for the road. Each.

Dom and I laughed our way through the loft to leave, and on our way out I hear someone say, "Hi Scott!" I look, and it's Michael Stipe. I didn't really know Michael Stipe, but we had been introduced a few times and it was cool he remembered my name (and that is not a dig at Dave). I was happy to see Michael, and I was happy to be drunk. Really drunk. High tolerance for all things booze, be damned drunk. I was a stupid, stumbling, laughing, happy drunk. When I drank I was like the happy Hulk: THE MORE SCOTT DRINKS THE HAPPIER SCOTT GETS!!!

"HI MICHAEL!!! HAPPY HOLIDAYS!" I yelled back at him, and then I bro-punched him in the arm very hard. REALLY hard.

There was a stunned silence around us after I socked him. My brain was lounging in a five-star resort's pool filled with vodka, and somewhere in there it understood that punching him like that was not cool. But like I said, I was the happy Hulk, and Bruce Banner was definitely not in control.

"Why did you do that?" Michael quietly asked as he rubbed his upper arm, clearly annoyed at me.

"BECAUSE EVERYBODY HURTS! SORRY MICHAEL STIPE! HAPPY HOLIDAYS!" I shouted as Dominick pulled me away and then out the door and down the steps and into the street and into a cab and off to some other spot, laughing our asses off 'til the break of dawn.

SORRY NEVER FELT SO GOOD

NYC Suite, Part Two

"You're not on the list. No, sorry, you're not on the list. Again, there's nothing I can do because you're Not. On. The. List."

I took such joy in the words my friend Joe inflicted on people on a nightly basis, each word leaving a mark on its wincing victim as if the dead-calm delivery of his message was a tiny blade flicking at their skin.

As doorman at a place called Moomba in New York City in the late 1990s, Joe was one of the most powerful men in the city. If you wanted in to what was *the* place to be, to see and be seen, to rub shoulders with the glitterati, to hang with supercool Danny DeVito, to get hit on by Lauren Holly (*Dumb and Dumber*), to bump into Bruce Willis in a stairway and have him say to you, "Someone is going to get the shit kicked out of them tonight," and you respond, "I hope it's not me," and he says, "No, not you, pal," and then he smiles and offers to buy you a drink—if you wanted to get into that room and be able to brag to your friends the next day that you got in, you had to get past Joe. It didn't matter if you were Mayor Giuliani, if Joe didn't give the nod to unhook the velvet rope, you were exiled, relegated to the dreary nowhere of 7th Avenue South.

Moomba was one of those New York City nightclubs that burn white hot for a time and then, poof, it's gone, leaving everybody with a story about how they used to hang out there with

DiCaprio and a gaggle of supermodels. Well, you didn't, because Joe wouldn't let you in.

My friend Dominick (who you may remember from such stories in this book like "Everybody Hurts") and I knew Joe from when he worked the door at Spy Bar, which was Moomba's predecessor in the canon of New York City lounge culture, catering to celebrities, models, trust-fund kids, starving artists, jerk-offs, and Wall Street types. On any given night we'd be drinking with the most eclectic range of characters. From Derek Jeter and Mariah Carey to Prince to Jerry Seinfeld (who told me he always thought Anthrax was the best name for a heavy metal band) to Salman Rushdie. Yes, Salman Rushdie, fresh on the Ayatollah's hit list, hanging out with us at Spy Bar, telling us about how he stays under the radar. As I sat there with Salman I couldn't help but think of how ironic it would be if I were to kill him and then the whole extremist Muslim world would have a Jew as a hero.

I was drunk.

Joe was a metalhead and skater and so were Dom and I, so we hit it off immediately. Most nights at Spy Bar I would hang outside with Joe and watch while he worked his magic at the door. I would stand back in the shadows of the doorway and observe this absurd sociological theater unfold as people would say or do anything to scam their way in. The nightly ritual was more fascinating than being in the actual bar. It was on one of those nights that Joe told me he was leaving Spy to work at the soon-to-open Moomba. Joe said, "It's going to be the spot, even more exclusive than Spy. Smaller, cooler, and you guys are always welcome." It was hard for me to imagine a place more fancy-pants than Spy Bar, and I asked Joe, "Really? How can you top this place?" Joe gave me his serious you're-not-getting-in-here-tonight-or-any-night look and said coyly, "You'll see."

Moomba opened in November of 1997, and the third floor VIP lounge, the mecca of New York City nightlife, quickly became our private clubhouse. It became the go-to spot for the A-list because nobody bothered them once they were inside. There were rules: no pictures, no autographs. It was a place to hang where your privacy mattered. And then there was Dom and me: "We were in that joint twenty-four hours a day. I mean another fucking few minutes, we could be stools, that's how often we were in there," to quote Sonny Bunz from *Goodfellas*. A typical night would go until 4 a.m., and then they'd kick everyone out, and Dom and I would hang after hours with Joe and his crew. Around six in the morning one of the cooks would make breakfast for everyone, and then I'd go back to my apartment and sleep until 4 p.m. and then start all over.

On most nights at Moomba I'd spend some time outside, hanging behind Joe, watching the tragicomic play unfold. Sometimes that's all I'd do, just come hang outside and then take off. The door scene was so much better than it was at Spy Bar. Moomba was smaller, and even more people wanted in. Oh the drama! The depths that people would mine for entry knew no bottom. Everybody had a story, everybody knew someone, everybody had a publicist who was supposed to get them in, everybody spoke to the owner and he put them on the list (the owner was Joe's brother Jeff, and no, he didn't), everybody was full of shit. So much talking and talking and talking and begging and pleading and even genuflecting at Joe and he would stand there aloof, filtering all the garbage being spewed at him. His quietly polite mantra of "You're not on the list. No, sorry, you're not on the list" falling on the deaf ears of the hopefully hopeless.

I noticed that the talkers rarely got in. If you approached the rope and started into some story, it wasn't going to happen. It was the people who didn't say anything who would get the nod from Joe, and the sea would part and the bells would chime and the gates of Valhalla would open and they'd be swept into paradise. Sometimes people would see me lurking in the background and start pleading their case to me, as if I had any power over the gates of Valhalla. I'd just slowly shake my head no, shrug my shoulders, and deflect them back to Joe.

The door of Moomba wasn't like Studio 54 in the seventies, with a coke-addled Steve Rubell creating a scene every night. Joe wasn't selecting people, and he was never a dick about turning people away. You were either on his radar or you weren't. He knew what and who worked in that room, and he curated it perfectly.

"You want to go work the door for a few?" Joe asked me late one night.

"Hell yeah! You know I've always wanted to do that," I happily replied. We were eating dinner at a table that had a view of the door (if you pulled back the curtain) so Joe would be able to peek out and keep an eye on me in case anything went awry. I'd also be able to look to him in case I wasn't sure about letting someone in. Joe told me to "just use your gut and have fun."

I zipped up my leather, pulled my hat down low, and headed out to the front line. I had a clipboard in hand with the guest list on it. It made for a nice prop—there was no list. It was pretty late, and things had already quieted down outside (but were raging inside), so I wouldn't be in the thick of it. After about ten minutes of nothing a limo rolled up and a guy—well dressed, early twenties, ubiquitous Patrick Bateman hairdo—gets out of the limo. He's obviously drunk and is talking loudly and very rudely to a woman who is still in the car. "Get out of the car. Will you just get the fuck out of the car!? What the fuck is your problem? Get out of the car," he whined. The woman eventually gets out of the car, and Mr. Manners grabs her by the upper arm and pulls her with him toward me, saying, "C'mon, COME ON, would you? Jesus Christ!" I pretend not to notice.

"I'm on the list," he says without breaking stride as if I'm going to unhook the rope and let him pass. I stand there silently staring at the traffic wheeling down 7th Avenue, and I definitely don't make any move to let them in. Annoyed, he repeats himself, "I'm ON the list." I slowly turn my head and deliberately lock eyes with the guy. He immediately averts his eyes, which tells me he's full of shit and I've won the battle. I'm going with my gut: this guy is not getting in. In my peripheral vision I could see the curtain move by the table where Joe was inside sitting and watching.

Again the guy says, "I'm on the list," but slightly less arrogant this time. I give his lady a smile that says, *You seem nice—you should make better choices*, and then I look at him and quietly speak the sacred words: "I'm sorry. You're not on the list." Gut-punched by the denial and embarrassed in front of the lady, he attempts to up his game by dropping a name. "Do you know who I am? Do you? I'm Paul Michaels, Lorne Michaels's son." He stands there, triumphant, waiting for me to let him in, apologize, do something, but I don't. I'm back to silently staring out at the cars on 7th Avenue, not a care in the world. Infuriated, he yells, "Hey asshole! Did you hear me? I'm Lorne Michaels's son. I come here all the time, and you'd better let me in!" I very slowly lift the clip-board up and give it a once over. I even turn a page, making it look like I'm actually looking for his name on the list. Again, there is no list. This is me having fun now because he called me an asshole. While I'm doing my slo-mo list check he's talking angrily under his breath to the woman loud enough for me to hear: "I'll call my father right now. This guy has no idea who he's dealing with. One call and this guy is fired." Then in his best pissy voice he says to me, "Are you finished checking? Did you find my name? I know it's on there. Jeff and Joe always have me on the list."

"I'm sorry, but you're not on the list," I quietly reiterated, and I walked back a few steps away from him, signaling I was done engaging. This drove him fucking crazy and he yelled, "DON'T YOU FUCKING IGNORE ME! THAT'S IT! I'M CALLING MY DAD. YOU'RE IN DEEP SHIT NOW, ASSHOLE!"

It was hard for me to stifle the giggles trying to escape. I stood there stone-faced, no reaction to his outburst at all, which made him even angrier. "WHAT THE FUCK? ARE YOU REALLY GO-ING TO MAKE ME CALL MY FATHER?" he yelled, shaking his phone at me.

I calmly replied, "Do what you need to do," as I let someone else in who I knew had walked up during his last attempt at yelling his way in. That was the last straw for him: "You let that guy in? Who the fuck was that guy? How does that guy just get in?" And then, ramping up: "Maybe you didn't hear me: I'M LORNE MI-CHAELS'S SON. HE'S MY DAD. DO YOU KNOW WHO LORNE MICHAELS IS?!"

I waited a beat, and then another, and then I smiled and said, "Yes, I know who Lorne Michaels is. And if he were here, I'd let *him* in"—dramatic pause—"*You* will never get in." And then I turned and walked back inside the bar, leaving LORNE MI-CHAELS'S SON to his own devices.

Joe was standing there with a huge smile on his face and yelled, "Yeahhhh, Scott Ian! That was the shit!" And we shook hands with a loud clap. "I was watching you through the curtain. You handled that guy perfectly."

"Wow, that fucking guy. What a dick," I said, shaking my head. "I can't believe the shit he was saying. Did he really think that calling me an asshole was going to get him in?" And then I asked the million-dollar question: "Was he really Lorne Michaels's son?"

Joe said, "Hell no. That guy always comes around trying to get in here. He's a jerk-off. Fuck him."

I sat back down at the table where a celebratory drink was waiting for me. I had passed the test. I peeked out the curtain to see if the guy was still standing there fulminating, but he was gone. There was just Joe, sentinel-like, keeping the naked city safe, one night at a time.

MARRIED WITH CHILDREN

"Did you have sex with Kelly Bundy?"

Over the last twenty-five years that question is easily in the top five questions I get asked. What's number-one, you ask? C'mon, that's easy. Have you been paying attention at all? Number one is, "Aren't you the lead singer of Anthrax?"

Duh.

Back to Kelly Bundy and whether or not I slept with her. You'd think that would be an easy question to answer, it's direct, no bullshit, straight to the point, right? On paper, yes, but in reality this question has many, many levels to it.

Let's break it down.

What this question proposes is that, first off, I had the balls to ask Christina Applegate on a date. Yes, like every other dude watching that show in 1992 I had a crush on her based on her looks, but in no way does that enable me to somehow ask her out as we made casual conversation around the craft service table while Anthrax was on set that week. Can you imagine? "Uhhh hi, Christina. Umm sooo yeah, uh . . . you like celery sticks too?" Nope, not going to happen. Take David Faustino to a Metallica show and get him wasted and watch the crowd chant, "BUD BUD BUD!" at him and then get admonished the next day by one of the producers because David was late to set and we'd better not do that again? Yes, I could do that. But ask Christina out? No fucking way.

But this is Hollywood, right? Where dreams are made reality and fantasies come to life (cough bullshit cough). Let's just say for the purpose of analyzing this question that I did ask her out and we had a really nice time at the La Brea Tar Pits—we "hit it off," as they say—and we decided to see each other again. We go out again and have another great time together at the Magic Castle, and after a few more dates we finally kiss. She's been wondering if I was ever going to kiss her, but I am such the gentleman. And then we start to see each other every day and really enjoy each other's company and talk on the phone when we're not together and go out every night, and then on one of those nights we end up back at my hotel room and are all over each other before I can even get the door open. We stumble into the room, pulling at each other's clothes, falling onto the bed mentally and physically locked in this intense moment of lust and right at the point of no return I stop and ask her if she'd fuck me as Kelly Bundy.

That's what that question proposes, that I asked Christina Applegate to fuck me in character, and by proposing that it is saying that I am an asshole and a creepy weirdo jerk, and if I did that, I would be. Because how else could I have had sex with Kelly Bundy? Sure, if she had initiated the whole thing in character, I would've went with it—who wouldn't?

But she didn't and I didn't and this whole Hollywood scenario I just made up is because people ask stupid questions and I stupidly can't simply answer the question with a no because the whole idea is ridiculous. People, there is no Kelly Bundy. She is a character Christina Applegate played on TV. So from now on the question should be: Did you have sex with Christina Applegate?

Now here is where the lines really start to blur.

When we first got the script for the episode "My Dinner with Anthrax," there was a scene where we were all hanging out in the Bundy living room, stuck inside because of a blizzard, and at some point after we had eaten from the "mystery pack" (if you've seen the episode, you know what I am talking about; if not, look it up on YouTube), Kelly takes my hand and walks me upstairs to her bedroom. She wants to hook up with a band guy. It turns out that band guy was me, and I was stoked.

I was the guy who would get to have sex with Kelly Bundy! Fake, make-believe sitcom sex! There wasn't even really a bedroom. The stairs that they would walk up to go to the second floor of their house didn't go anywhere. There was no second floor. Just some other stairs on the other side of the fake wall to walk back down. Even though everything about it was fake, I was still happy to be the guy.

It was Monday, our first day on set, and when we did the read-through with the cast everything went really well and the scene where Kelly and I walk upstairs together got a big salacious "Oooooooohhhh" in the room. On Tuesday we did another table read, and I noticed there were some changes in the script but not for me. All my lines were the same. The cast members were really cool and supportive and would help us get our lines right. You'd think it'd be easy to play yourself. It's not. It's awkward saying lines that aren't yours if you're not an actor. I asked Ed O'Neill (Al Bundy) how he gets into character because it seemed so easy for him. One minute you'd be talking to Ed, and the next he'd be Al. In real life Ed is nothing like Al. You have to be very smart to play that dumb. Ed said, "Scott, as soon as I put on Al's dirty white undershirt I become the character. That's all I need."

On Wednesday we did another read, with more changes in other people's lines, but all my stuff was still intact. We rehearsed for the first time on the set, and I could see the show coming together. We also got to use the breakaway bottles for the first time. There's something very satisfying about smashing a glass bottle over someone's head. We went nuts with the breakaway stuff, throwing glasses at each other, smashing lamps with guitars, breaking bottles over our own heads until a producer told us to quit it because that stuff costs a lot to make. I want a whole house made of breakaway materials.

The production moved very quickly. They'd only started on Monday, and by Friday they would have a new episode done. We were surrounded by pros, and we were losing our minds over being a part of something so cool. We were all huge fans of *Married with Children*, and to be a part of it was surreal. We were actually in an episode. What an amazing mind-fuck that was. And it all happened because we asked Missi Callazzo from Megaforce Records to call Fox and try to get us on *The Simpsons*. We wanted Anthrax on that show, and Missi would call all the time. Eventually she got a call back from a producer telling her he had a script that needed a band, not from *The Simpsons* but from *Married with Children*, and would Anthrax be interested? Hell yes, we would.

We got to the studio Thursday, and the script guy handed me the new version. I started reading through to see if anything had changed, and the whole scene where Kelly takes my hand and walks me upstairs was gone. Damn. I found one of the producers we were dealing with and told him I had just read through the script and my big scene was cut. He told me that after we were finished reading on Wednesday Christina asked them to take that scene out. I was bummed and asked if he knew why. He told me Christina was uncomfortable with it and said, "I know my character is a slut. She's just not that much of a slut."

End scene.

I was bummed, but I got over it, as it was Friday now and we were going to be taping the show in front of a live audience. And I still had my, "Duh cuhliz, duh cuhliz" (take away my then thick NY accent and I was saying, "The colors, the colors") line after I ate from the mystery pack and was tripping. The taping went great, and we all got big laughs in the right places, especially at the end when we played "In My World" and destroyed their living room. Smashing up the Bundys' house with Kelly, Bud, and Marcie is one of the best things I have ever done.

Oh, and the answer to the question is *no*.

And we still haven't been on *The Simpsons*.

THE WRATH OF KIRK

"'Only' is a perfect song," said James (Hetfield, for those of you who are reference challenged—there's only one James). "It's perfect. You guys were great tonight." James was sitting on a road case in the downstairs catering area backstage at the Warfield Theater in San Francisco, and we were chatting post-Anthrax show. To have James, the guy who wrote "Master of Puppets," for fuck's sake, say that a song we worked so hard on was perfect, well, that was awesome. "Only" was so important to the band at that time; it was the song that introduced John Bush as our new singer and became an anthem for us in 1993–1994 on the Sound of White Noise tour. James, Lars, and Kirk had come down to see the show and hang out with us, and they had just witnessed a rager of a gig.

I wholeheartedly thanked James over and over for the compliments, and talk of the show quickly turned into talk about what we were doing after the show. Lars and Kirk suggested we all go to the notorious landmark San Francisco strip club the O'Farrell Theatre. San Francisco is Metallica's town, so we were in for whatever shenanigans they had planned. There was a well-oiled crew of us heading out into the Tenderloin: John, Charlie, Frankie, and I along with James, Lars, Kirk, Mark Osegueda from Death Angel, and Steve Wiig (who at the time worked for Lars and was the sober driver). We caravanned to the O'Farrell in Lars's car and a taxi, all of us loud, buzzed, and ready for what felt like a night out in 1986 when we were a bunch of kids ignorant of the fact that the world was about to open its doors to our music. We were just having fun with old friends.

We barreled into the O'Farrell and did some damage. To our livers.

James, Lars, and Kirk were surprised by how much us Anthrax guys were drinking. They knew us as a bunch of practically sober dudes—compared to them, anyway. Back in the eighties, when some called them Alcoholica, we were Soberthrax, the kings of beer nursing. Things had changed since the eighties, and at this point in 1994 I was in my living-in-NYC-out-all-night-drinking mode and was proud of it. We were tearing it up hard at the O'Farrell, the strippers coming in a distant second to the booze-soaked revelry. At some point during this drinking melee Kirk told me he had to split. He was dealing with the end of a relationship, breaking up with his girlfriend, and he had to go home to have "the talk." He was really bummed to have to leave us—we hadn't all been together like this in a long time. We all tried to convince him not to go, but I could tell this was weighing on him; he wasn't his usual happy self. We all drunkenly hugged him goodnight and Kirk left and we got back to the business at hand, which was trying to drink all the booze at the O'Farrell. At around 3 a.m. everyone stumbled out onto O'Farrell Street laughing and yelling and not wanting the night to end. *Someone* had the idea that we should jam—if we only had instruments and a place to go and play, it'd be so rad. Our Anthrax gear was all packed up, so that wasn't going to work. James and Lars didn't live in the city and it'd be too far to drive, so that wasn't going to work either. But we kept on it, our drunken grip on jamming not letting go. The hive-mind had taken over. Then *someone* else said, "Hey, Kirk has a studio in his house and he lives in the city!" (I'm not putting someone in italics because I don't want to name names—I'll name every name. I don't remember who initially floated the idea of jamming or mentioned that Kirk had a studio. It may have been me. If it was, I own it.) And then Mark said, "I know the code to the alarm to get in," and that was it. We were going to Kirk's house. There was a lot of yelling and wild-eyed smiling and someone shouted, "Let's get beer to bring with us!" And if I remember correctly, we bought beer from the strip club to go.

Somewhere in the way back of my brain a warning light was going off. I remembered Kirk telling me why he had to leave earlier, what he had to deal with, and I thought maybe it wasn't a good idea for all of us drunks to show up at his house expecting to play really loud music, so I told everybody why Kirk left, but it didn't make a dent in our mission to make metal.

On the way to Kirk's house Frankie decided to make room for more booze and released a torrent of puke all over the floor of the backseat of Lars's Range Rover. Then he emptied more on the inside of the door, puking into the door handle and cup holder. Finally he was able to open the window and vomit out of the car all the rest of the way to Kirk's. Lars seemed quite amused by the whole mess, almost like he was happy that things were getting so nuts, and he was busting Frankie's balls about being a lightweight. Compared to those guys, we all were.

We got to Kirk's house in Pacific Heights, and we all got very quiet for a second. It was the middle of the night, and we were all standing in the middle of the street, mansions looming over us from every direction. This was some covert shit we were about to do, and we were very serious about it, earnest in the way only the really intoxicated can be.

Mark would lead the way, as he had the keys to the kingdom, and we would stealthily follow until we were in the safety of Kirk's studio, where we could fire up the amps and bash out some shitty Sabbath.

And then all of us were clumsily walking up Kirk's steep driveway and around the back of the house, giggling like little kids and loudly shushing each other, which caused us to laugh even harder.

Mark was opening the door and we were walking into Kirk's house, down the steps to the basement and down a hallway and into his studio jam room. Someone (yep, someone again) locked the door behind us, and within seconds of us walking into the studio we were plugging in guitars and amps and cracking open beers and it was on. Had Kirk heard us come in? None of us cared. We launched into playing Sabbath and Maiden and Priest and Motörhead really, really loud and, mind you, not very well. We kept trading instruments, like we were having a competition to see who could play the worst, which made it all the more fun. James was playing drums and Charlie was playing guitar and we were all in drunken metal heaven. We decided to trade instruments again, and I got on the drums and we were plowing our way through some song, probably something Sabbath, when I happened to look up and see Kirk's face frantically staring at me through the porthole window in the door to the studio. I could see that he was trying to open the door, but we had locked it from the inside. He kept looking down toward the doorknob on his side of the door and then back up through the window, where only I could see him because everyone else had their backs to the door. I pretended I didn't see him. I didn't want to stop playing—it was just too much fun. He was getting even more frenzied now; I could see the panic in his eyes, and he was shaking his head back and forth for us to stop. I kept pounding out a beat, and James and Charlie and Frankie were playing away, laughing and headbanging. Kirk started making the universal sign for "cut" by dragging his index finger across his throat. He desperately wanted us to stop playing, and I continued to ignore him for another minute or two and then finally I looked up at him with a smiley look of, *Oh hey, buddy, I didn't see you out there*, and I stopped drumming. That caused the other guys to stop playing, and when they looked over at me to see why I stopped I pointed over to the door where Kirk was now angrily staring at us and banging on the door yelling, "OPEN THIS DOOR RIGHT NOW! OPEN THIS FUCKING DOOR!"

We opened the door. Someone, whomever was closest to it, opened it, and Kirk came screaming into the room, "HOW DARE YOU?! HOW DARE YOU?! HOW DARE YOU DO THIS? YOU BROKE INTO MY HOUSE?! THIS IS A VIOLATION, YOU FUCKING ASSHOLES! HOW DARE YOU?!?!?! THIS IS NOT FUCKING COOL!!!"

Silence.

Just seconds earlier the cacophony of noise we were making was deafening, and now there was complete silence in the wake of Kirk screaming at us. I got up from behind the drums, banging into them as I stood up, making a loud noise, and that set Kirk off again. "COME ON, GUYS! WHAT THE FUCK? DID YOU THINK IT WAS OKAY TO BREAK INTO MY HOUSE? DID YOU?!"

No one replied. We were all just standing around like a bunch of delinquents who had been sent to the principal's office, heads lowered, glancing at each other and trying not to laugh. Yes, we were that much a bunch of assholes. Here is our friend, our brother, completely flipping out, absolutely furious at us for this stunt we have pulled, and all we can do is stand there and try not to giggle. None of us had ever seen or heard Kirk like this. Never. And when he was yelling at us, repeating, "HOW DARE YOU!" his voice would get higher. I had my head down, staring at my sneakers as he rightfully berated us, and I saw James's face, wide-eyed with surprise and on the verge of cracking up, and that made me start laughing, but I held it in, trying not to let Kirk see. Lars was trying to keep it together, giving serious looks to anyone who was smiling but then almost losing it himself. It was a really uncomfortably hilarious scene, awkward, to say the least.

Kirk had started to ramp down and, with that calming, was able to see we were not taking things very seriously. "You guys think this is funny?" he said quietly with a disappointed tone like your dad would. "You think it's funny to break into my house and do this? You think it's okay to violate the sanctity of my house? It shows no respect for me, just complete disrespect. I'm upstairs dealing with personal issues, and you guys break in here and just start playing like it's okay to do that? I could feel the vibrations all the way upstairs. I thought someone had really broken in, and I walk into this? This is my house. Just no fucking respect."

We all started to apologize: "Sorry, man. We're really sorry. Shit. Sorry, bro. We respect you . . ."

Kirk just stared at us all standing there, heads down, shuffling our feet, just wanting this to be over, and he said, "Get out of my house. Now. Get out."

We all started to move toward the door, mumbling more lame apologies—"Sorry, dude. We didn't mean to. Bro, we're really sorry . . ."

And Kirk just repeated, "Get out."

Shell-shocked for the moment from the chastising we had received, we walked silently in a line out of the studio, down the hallway, back up the steps, out the door, and down Kirk's steep driveway, and as soon as we were in the street and the moment of gravitas wore off, the tension broke by Charlie saying, "He just yelled at us," and we all started cracking up—so much for respecting the sanctity of his house. We were all standing in the middle of the street out in front of his house, reenacting the scene over and over, taking turns as Kirk yelling. We couldn't get enough—the whole scenario was so ridiculous and, in the moment, drunk at 5 a.m., hilarious.

The frivolity eventually died down, and we started to talk about what to do next: we weren't going to stand in the middle of the street until sunrise—we needed a plan. There were still bars open if we wanted to go that route. Then our drunk hive-mind kicked in again, and we got it into our heads that we needed to apologize to Kirk again. Yes! That's what we needed to do! We had majorly disrespected our bro and we had to say we were sorry!

Oh boy.

We all thought this was a great idea, but no one wanted to be the one to walk up to Kirk's front door and ring the bell. We were scared! Lars said he would go but Frankie had to come with him. Frankie said he would, and the two of them walked up the steps to Kirk's front door, leaving the rest of us out in the street, anxiously watching. Lars and Frankie got to the door and pushed the button on the intercom. No answer. They started knocking on Kirk's massive wood door framed in glass. No answer. They kept ringing his intercom, calling his name—"Kirk! Kirk! HEY KIRK!"—getting louder and louder, knocking harder and harder, and then *CRACK*. "What the hell was that?" I said, looking around at everyone else. "Shit, what was that?"

We had heard a really loud cracking sound, and then Lars hissed down to us, "Frankie kicked the door."

Oh shit.

And as if on cue, there was Kirk leaning out a second-story window above the front door yelling, "WHAT DID YOU DO TO MY DOOR? WHAT THE FUCK ARE YOU GUYS DOING?"

Lars and Frankie were both nervously answering at the same time, "We were trying to get you on the intercom. We wanted to say we were sorry again. You weren't answering. Uhh, I kicked the door."

Kirk said, "I didn't answer because it's FIVE O'CLOCK IN THE FUCKING MORNING! WOULD YOU GUYS JUST GET THE HELL OUT OF HERE?!" And then he disappeared from the window. Lars and Frankie started to turn to come back down the steps, and then we heard Kirk yelling from inside the house, "YOU BROKE MY DOOR! YOU FUCKING BROKE MY DOOR!" Lars and Frankie scrambled down the steps, and we all started running, the whole mess of us piling into Lars's car to get the hell out of there. Better to deal with a pukey car than facing the wrath of Kirk again. As we were pulling away I turned and could see Kirk out on the landing in front of his door looking at it.

Stunned by this last development we decided that the evening's festivities were done and us Anthrax guys would go back to our hotel. The topic of conversation turned to why did Frankie kick the door? Nobody had an answer—it was just a spur-of-the-moment thing and that was that, our amazing night ended with a *CRACK*. We had committed vandalism and a home invasion—two felonies. Not bad for a night out. The sun was coming up as we said our good-byes and I hit my bed hard, asleep on impact, good-night . . .

. . . and then the wake-up call that our tour manager had so responsibly set for our rooms shocked me awake and the night before came hurtling back at me like a thirty-gallon Hefty bag filled with tomatoes and milk dropped from the fiftieth floor of a high-rise onto the roof of a building forty-four stories below, *BOOM!*

(I may or may not have witnessed that happen once.)

I had to call Kirk. I was feeling intense guilt for what we had done to him, and I had to apologize. I hoped he'd even talk to me. I wouldn't have blamed him if he never spoke to me again. I ran down to the lobby and grabbed a coffee to clear my head (the epic hangover hadn't kicked in yet) and then called him. Kirk answered, and I dove right into my apology. I was truly sorry. I felt terrible about what we had done, and I hoped I could make it up to him somehow.

He thanked me and then said, "Man, I'm sorry too. I'm sorry for yelling at you guys. I was dealing with breaking up with my girlfriend, and that was going really shitty, and then I could hear you guys playing, and all I wanted to do was get away from her and come jam with you guys and have fun, but she went nuts, yelling about how could I let my friends take advantage of me, blah blah blah, and I just wanted to be in that room with you guys. Anyway, we're broken up now, so at least that's done."

Wow. I was shocked. I had no idea he was feeling that way. He really acted the part of the violated homeowner really well. I apologized again, and he said it really was unnecessary, no worries. He'd already spoken to Lars and James, and everything was fine. I thanked him for being so cool and such a good friend. Kirk really is the best. I told him how the whole plan went down, how when he was yelling at us we were trying so hard not to just fall down laughing. He knew—he was trying not to laugh as well. We were laughing on the phone talking about it, and then he brought up his door. It really was broken. There was a big crack in the glass part that framed the wood. He had a guy coming to look at it to give him an estimate to fix it. The door was imported from Italy, and it was expensive. I apologized again; even though I hadn't actually kicked the door, I was definitely an accomplice. Kirk wasn't bothered at all; he'd get it fixed. I jokingly said, "You should send the bill to Frankie."

Kirk said, "That's a great idea! What a great wind-up that would be! I'll do it."

I told Charlie and John what was happening so we'd all be in on it and really make Frankie believe he was going to have to pay.

Charlie, John, and I set it up so Frankie would "overhear" us talking about the bill for the door. We were hanging in the dressing room a few days after the San Francisco incident, and I mentioned how I had spoken to Kirk that day and he was getting the estimate to fix his door and how the door was a very expensive one-of-a-kind handmade door from Italy and only a few people in the United States could even work on it. Frankie was starting to sweat. Then Charlie would pick up the thread and say he spoke to

Kirk, who told him he was sending the bill over to our management to pay for the repairs. The parts had to be imported, and it was going to be pricey. Frankie was starting to freak. This all led up to Frankie talking to Kirk, who told him he expected Frankie to pay for the repair, as it was only fair, and that he'd fax the bill over. Frankie agreed—he really didn't have a choice. He was bummed out about what he did and scared over what he was going to be on the hook for. The next day Kirk faxed a repair invoice for $16,000. Frankie was flipping out! Sixteen grand to fix the door! We were all laughing about the great wind-up and at the same time commiserating with him; he was really losing it over having to pay that much money for a drunken mistake. He started making arrangements to get Kirk the money. Kirk let Frankie sweat it for a few days, sending gentle reminders about the money, and when Frankie had reached his apex of frustration and stress Kirk, being the nice guy he is, let him off the hook. To say Frankie was relieved would've been the understatement of the decade. That's when we should've had Lars send over the bill to clean his car.

A LESSON IN ~~VIOLENCE~~ ENGLISH

It was a beautiful southern California day, and I was driving (speeding) on the Pacific Coast Highway, cranking Slayer's *Reign in Blood* album in my car, yelling along with Tom Araya on the middle bridge of "Angel of Death" (as one does):

> Seas of blood, bury life, smell your death as it burns deep
> inside of you.
> Abacinate, eyes that bleed, praying for the end of your wide
> awake nightmare.

Yep, just yelling along like I have since 1986 when I first bought *Reign in Blood* and listened on headphones in my tiny room in my mom's apartment. Just yelling along like I have at the countless Slayer shows I have seen over the last thirty years, whether I was in the mosh pit or stagediving or from the safety of my dressing room backstage when we've been on tour together, always just yelling along. So after all this time I have been singing along with Slayer it was quite something to realize that I had no idea what Tom was saying. Seriously, I had to stop the car, pull over, and scan back on my phone to hear the word again. How could there be a word in that bridge that I have been yelling for thirty years and have no idea what it means?

The word is *abacinate*.

Abacinate? I can't tell you how many times I've yelled that word. Abacinate! What the fuck does *abacinate* mean?

If only there were a device . . .

I Googled *abacinate*.

abacinate: To blind by holding a red-hot metal rod or plate before the eyes.

Pleasant.

Leave it to Jeff Hanneman to go the extra mile lyrically for "Angel of Death," to actually do the research and come up with a verb that gives us a brutal window into the horrors of Auschwitz that he so eloquently describes in his vivid prose.

Jeff, sly wordsmith that he was, actually hints at the definition in the lyric because the line after the word *abacinate* is "Eyes that bleed."

I had never heard of it before, and I consider myself to be very well versed in the ways of torture (I read a lot of horror). It was Jeff's lyric that caused me to look up abacinate and learn something new and horrible! And now you know it too! Thanks, Professor Ian.

Upon learning this fun new word I thought back to when I was a kid in grade school and how, when I would learn a new word in class, I would have to get up in front of the classroom and give the definition of the word and then spell that word and then use it in a sentence. I've already given the definition, and you can see how to spell it, so I would say to you, my readers, "Abacinate. I would rather abacinate myself than listen to Kanye West."

So the next time you're with your friends somewhere drinking and listening to Slayer and "Angel of Death" comes on, you can impress them with this new addition to your lexicon.

"Hey guys! You know what that word *abacinate* means? That word that Tom just yelled?" And your friends will most likely reply, "Shut the fuck up. We're listening to Slayer."

After having this learning experience through metal I was curious and wanted more. Knowledge is power! I listened intently to my Slayer catalog and came up with a few more gems of the English language that I thought I would share with you.

Disapprobation. There's a word I wasn't using conversationally. It's from the song "Criminally Insane": *"Disapprobation, what have I done? I have yet only just begun to take your fuckin' lives."*

Disapprobation means *"the state of disapproving, or disapproval."* Jeff and Kerry are writing about a killer who is saying to those who would keep him/her incarcerated, "Yeah? You disapprove of me, motherfuckers? I've only just started to murder you assholes! You fuckin' think I'm finished? Fuck that shit! When I get out of here you're all dead!!!"

And to use it in a sentence: "Last year Angus Young was in a state of extreme disapprobation over Phil Rudd."

And speaking of Phil Rudd, while we are in a state of learning, let me give you a little tip in life: if you're the drummer of AC/DC, don't do meth and threaten people.

My next vocabularial treasure is the word *modulistic* from the song "Piece by Piece": *"Modulistic terror, a vast sadistic feast. The only way to exit is going piece by piece."* Modulistic? I know the word *module*. I know the word *modular*. I know a lot of words. Modulistic? Not so much, so I looked it up. I used an actual dictionary and could not find the word *modulistic*. Weird.

Then I Googled it and got results that seemed like the definition of the word *modulistic*: *"A standardized, often interchangeable component of a system or construction that is designed for easy assembly or flexible use: a sofa consisting of two end modules."*

Nice try, Google, but that reads to me like the definition of a module or a modular system. I'm starting to think I need to call bullshit on modulistic. Then I clicked on the links for modulistic, and they took me to definitions of the word *module*. What conspiratorial web are you weaving, Internet? If you're trying to confuse me, you're doing a great job. Is it module or modulistic? Or maybe even the Internet doesn't know. Did I just beat the Internet?

After much investigation and some deep, deep contemplation, I decided that modulistic is not a real word.

Me and my favorite English professor, Dr. Hanneman.
Photo by Scott Ian.

I could not find a usage for it that modular wouldn't cover, except for in the lyrics to "Piece by Piece." Kerry King just knew that syllabically *modular* doesn't work where *modulistic* does. And aurally *modulistic* just sounds so much meaner. I'll have to ask Kerry someday after a few shots what he was thinking. Likely answer: "I don't know!"

Oh, and I almost forgot to use it in a sentence: "Modulistic is proof that Slayer are so cool they can make up words."

During my perusal of Slayer lyrics I came across another word I was not friends with in the song "South of Heaven":

Forgotten children, conform a new faith,
Avidity and lust controlled by hate.

Can you guess which word? I'll give you a hint: it's not hate.
Avidity means "extreme eagerness or enthusiasm."
Here's how I would use it in a sentence: "Slayer's avidity to the idea of sending assholes and jerks to hell is quite apparent in the lyrics to 'South of Heaven.'"

That's our lesson for today, my friends. I hope you enjoyed expanding your vocabularies to the sweet sounds of Slayer. See how fun learning can be? If only high school English had been so engaging.

I'm the only nerd who thinks about this shit.

ALL-IN

Part One

Once upon a time I was a professional poker player.

Which for me is weird considering I never gamble. I actually have zero affinity for it, never have. Slots, blackjack (unless you're counting cards), craps, roulette—all sucker bets designed to take your money. The house isn't in business to pay out on a regular basis. Yes, everyone has had or knows someone who has had a lucky moment when they hit it big, but over time the house always wins, and I'm not in business to lose.

I've been going to Las Vegas since the 1980s on tour, and when the rest of our crew is running for the tables as fast as they can, I'm looking for somewhere good to eat. You can eat really well in Vegas. I would drop a grand on food and booze at Joël Robuchon any day of the week in lieu of watching it disappear into the hands of some dead-eyed dealer at a card table filled with yellow-fingered emphysema candidates. The epic meal becomes a gold-tinged memory for my lifetime. Losing a grand? That'd make me start smoking.

I'm not even just talking about gambling with money. I don't gamble on decisions in general. I am a meticulous planner and approach every situation in life the same way: I think it through with Spock-like logic using experience, instinct, and the information at hand for the best possible outcome. In other words, I like to win. I guess that's why I got along so well with poker.

And it all started because I wanted a free trip to Las Vegas. Who wouldn't? It was back in 2006, and I was still drinking somewhat heavily, not up to my late 1990s levels, but enough to warrant a couple of days in Vegas with Pearl on VH1's dime. Yes, VH1, the network that gave me a job hosting the *Rock Show* back in 2001 when I oh-so needed one and then kept me gainfully employed over the years after that as a talking head on their endless *I Love the . . .* programs and assorted other list shows as well as casting me on their reality show *SuperGroup*, which was shot in Vegas earlier that year. VH1 was having a poker tournament, a "Rock & Roll" no-limit Texas hold 'em poker tournament in Vegas with Ace Frehley from Kiss, Dusty Hill from ZZ Top, Vinnie Paul from Pantera/HELLYEAH, Sully from Godsmack, as well as a couple of other players who would win their seats playing in a no-limit Texas hold 'em tournament on an online poker site called Ultimate Bet. I read about this tournament online on some metal news site. I barely knew how to play poker. As a kid I would play seven-card stud with my mom, and my memories of that were vague at best. I didn't know anything about online poker or no-limit Texas hold 'em. I just wanted a free ride out to Vegas for a few days to party. I emailed my friend Erik Luftglass; he was a bigwig in the talent department at VH1 and the man responsible for all the love I got from VH1. I asked him if I could be a part of the tournament, and he got back to me right away, saying he had spoken to Lisa Tenner (the producer of the show), and she thought it was a great idea to include me. Sweet! Three days in Vegas with my lady, raging with Vinnie Paul on VH1's tab. Perks! I neglected to tell him that I didn't know how to play hold 'em. I would need to do something about that, so I Googled no-limit Texas hold 'em for info on how to play. There were dozens of sites that had the basic rules. It seemed easy enough, but so much of the poker language they used—phrases like *under the gun, check-raise, gutshot straight, nuts, suckout*—I had no idea what they were talking about. Almost every article I read about learning Hold 'em pointed to Doyle Brunson's book

Super System as the go-to book to learn the basics. I got that and may as well have been trying to read ancient Sumerian. Pot odds and playing in or out of position and variance—I didn't have a clue. Reading wasn't cutting it for me. I needed to actually see how to play, to know what was going on, so I started watching the TV show *High Stakes Poker*, which was hosted by Gabe Kaplan (Mr. Kotter, to those of us in a certain age group) and my shotgun education in no-limit Texas hold 'em had begun.

Kind of. I didn't have time to sit around and watch poker on television all day. I watched two or three episodes and watched as poker pros won and lost huge amounts of money, literally hundreds of thousands of dollars. I couldn't believe how they could just lose so much money and be cool about it. They'd sit there casually chatting, as one guy would be stacking up a mountain of chips he had just won from the other guy. How could they do that? I would lose my sanity. Chat casually? I'd start hitting people with chairs screaming, "GIVE ME MY FUCKING MONEY BACK!!!" That's why I would never ever be in that position. I gleaned a bit of info from watching, basics like posting blinds and how the button moves around the table, but that was it. I really wasn't paying attention; I was just looking forward to a crazy few days in Vegas and that would be the end of poker in my world.

Crazy how things don't work out sometimes.

Pearl and I got to Vegas the day before the tournament. I was a little stressed about not knowing how to play and making a jackass out of myself, so we figured it would be a good idea to calm that by staying out all night drinking with Vinnie Paul and friends. It worked. I woke up the next day still drunk and not worried at all. My plan was to be out of the tournament right away and then to start drinking again to stave off the hangover and then go eat a fabulous meal somewhere. See how I thought that through logically? Always planning.

I had to be at the Flamingo Hotel at 10 a.m. for the tournament. Pearl, my partner in crime and trooper that she is, woke up with me after maybe three hours sleep, and we got our shit together and headed over to the Flamingo. They were going to shoot all of us band guys being tutored by poker professionals before the tournament.

Here's the thing: all the other guys playing were veteran poker players. Ace and Dusty had been playing since they were kids. Vinnie Paul is Vinnie Paul. He's a hard-charging drinking and gambling motherfucker. And Sully? Sully was practically a pro. He'd cashed in the main event of the 2006 World Series of Poker that summer, coming in 713th out of 8,773 people for $17,730. He'd go on to cash in the 2007 World Series as well, coming in 237th out of 6,358 people for $45,422, and then in December of 2007 he placed second out of 307 in the Doyle Brunson Five Diamond World Poker Classic $5,000 buy-in tournament for $307,325! Sully was badass. The other three guys playing with us were all players who won their seats by winning tournaments online, so they were all real dudes as well. Then there was me, sweating and still drunk from the night before, ordering a coffee and a Bloody Mary as soon as I walked into the studio: the extent of my poker knowledge? That pairs were good hands.

Double-fisting, I sat down with poker pro Antonio Esfandiari, aka "The Magician." He was and is a big deal. In 2012 Antonio won $18,346,673 at the World Series of Poker Big One for One Drop $1 million buy-in tournament. Yes, you read that correctly: He had the balls to put a million of his own money on the line, and he won over $18 million. In the tournament 11.11 percent of each buy-in would go to the One Drop charity, and they raised over $7 million from that one tournament.

Antonio asked me how often I played, and I lied and told him, "I played a lot on tour." He started right in, talking about raising

three-x to open and bet sizing and pot odds and a whole bunch of
other beginner stuff that I couldn't compute in my post-all-nighter,
pre-all-dayer state of mind. He ran a few hands with me, and I
was able to learn a few things, one of which was "raising three-x"
meant raising three times the amount of the big blind if everyone
folded before me and I was going to bet. So now I knew that and
having two aces was really good. After meeting with Antonio I
went to another room to get some instruction from Phil "The Unabomber" Laak, another big-deal poker pro. His nickname was the
Unabomber because he always wore a hoodie, making him look
like the police sketch of Ted Kaczynski. Phil was really friendly,
an affable guy. We joked around a bit and I told him I didn't know
how to play. He laughed it off and went over the same basics with
me that Antonio did. He wished me luck and then it was time to
shuffle up and deal. I was ready! Poker pros Phil Hellmuth Jr. and
Mark Tenner were hosting the tournament and would also be doing the play-by-play commentating. They introduced each player,
and we walked out onto the set through a dramatic cloud of some
fog-machine-generated smoke. Bloody Mary in hand, I took my
seat at the table.

Tournament director Matt Savage cried, "Shuffle up and
deal!" And we were underway. I was nervous. I sat there as hands
were dealt, and I kept folding: I didn't have anything even close
to a hand. Even with the buzz I had going, my nerves were on
fire. I was trying to talk myself down, my inside voice telling me,
*Just be cool. You got this. You're not even playing with your own
money—it's all for charity, so just chill and have fun. How hard can
it be?* I didn't even know that you were supposed to actually say
"bet" and "raise" when you were going to bet until I heard the
other players do so. I was very focused on the action. I made sure
to post my blinds when it was my turn so as not to hold up the
game. I made sure not to check, call, or fold out of turn. I started

getting used to the rhythm of the game and the basic mechanics, and I started to relax after a couple of rounds. I didn't look like an idiot. The Bloody Marys were helping as well. I was in some kind of new weird head place, the adrenaline from playing was counteracting the lack of sleep, and the drinks were kicking the shit out of any potential hangover. I felt good, really good. I was into the game, busting balls and having fun. Then I picked up a hand.

Okay, press pause for a second. I'm going to go into some detail about the hand, and I'll be using some poker terms/ phrases that I certainly didn't know back then and that you, my friendly reader, also may not know or understand, so I'll try to keep it all in layman's terms as much as I can. I'm not a poker writer anyway, and I don't know all the shorthand, so if you do know how to play and write out a hand history, pro-style, pretend you don't. Also, obviously at the time I didn't know people's hole cards, meaning I didn't know what cards they had. I watched it on TV and got to see after the fact. Oh and also, we couldn't hear Phil and Mark commenting on the game. Okay, press play . . .

FYI:

Blinds: blinds are forced bets posted by players to the left of the dealer button in flop-style poker games. The player to the left of the dealer button places the small blind and the next player to the left then posts the big blind.

Button: the dealer button is a marker used to indicate the player who is dealing or, in casino games with a house dealer, the player who acts last on that deal (who would be the dealer in a home game).

The blinds were $100/$200. Dusty Hill limps (meaning he just calls the amount of the big blind) with a ten and eight of diamonds (10d8d). Sully raises to $1,000 with a pair of nines, or pocket nines (99). I call Sully's nines with an ace of hearts and a six of hearts (Ah6h). Ace calls with a pair of fours, or pocket fours (44). The pot has $3,300 in it. The flop (the three community cards the dealer deals and then turns face up) comes ten of clubs (10c), ace of diamonds (Ad), and king of spades (Ks). I flop an ace, giving me top pair. This is very good for me—even I know that then. Ace acts first and checks. Sully bets $1,200, and then I raise to $2,400. Now it's Ace's turn. Phil Hellmuth says, "Ace Frehley has an easy fold, as he is a ten-to-one underdog." Phil knows how to calculate odds in poker like you and I can tell time on a digital clock. Ace either doesn't know that he's a ten-to-one underdog or doesn't care and calls the $2,400, making the pot $9,300. Sully folds. The turn card (the fourth card the dealer deals) is the queen of hearts (Qh). Phil says, "Ace is a twenty-to-one underdog. He needs a four on the river to beat Scott's pair of aces. I don't see how Ace can play if Scott bets." Looking very serious, Ace checks, poker face turned up to eleven. And then, like the novice I was, I check the turn as well. Terrible play—I should've bet. Phil even exclaims, "Ahhh, Scott!" If I bet, maybe I get Ace to fold his hand. My gut tells me now, after seeing it, that he was not folding no matter what I did. The dealer deals the river card (the fifth and last card dealt), and it is a four. Ace stoically bets $4,000, and I call, making the pot $17,300, and we turn our hands over and I see he made his set (three-of-a-kind) on the river. Ace only had two outs, meaning he could only win if one of the two fours left in the deck was dealt. It was, and I lost a lot of chips, almost crippling me early in the tournament.

I was now what was known as short stacked. I just knew I had enough chips for a few more rounds of blinds, and then I'd bust

Poker-face Ace crushes me. Courtesy Lisa Tenner.

out and be out the door and on my way to a big greasy breakfast
and a well-needed nap. I had no choice but to go all-in with whatever hand I had—it was shove or fold, meaning risking my tournament life every time I played a hand. Lucky for me, when I went
all-in, everyone else folded and I picked up the blinds. I was able
to pull that off a few times over the next hour or so as well as winning a couple of small pots as I slowly clawed back into the game.
I played as carefully as I could, which wasn't hard because I didn't
know what I was doing anyway, so I only played a hand if I had
one. I stayed very patient. I figured I'd let the rest of them battle
it out and knock each other out. That strategy wouldn't leave me
with a lot of chips at the end, but again, I didn't know this at the
time. I was in survival mode after almost busting out against Ace,
and I was going to last as long as I could. I got into another hand
with Ace; I had pocket twos, and he had an ace and a seven off suit
(meaning the two cards were of different suits). I bet every street
(meaning after the flop, the turn, and the river), and Ace called
me all the way down, and my pocket twos (aka ducks) held up. I
won some of my chips back to get my revenge, and my comeback
was in full swing.

Revenge of the ducks! Courtesy Lisa Tenner.

Vinnie Paul was the first player to get knocked out of the tournament, his three and six of spades (3s6s) flush draw falling short against Ace's A10.

One by one the other players got knocked out of the game, Sully doing most of the knocking. He busted Dusty Hill, his pair of jacks holding up against Dusty's A4. Dusty had been using a ZZ Top keychain as his card protector. Players will put a good luck charm on top of their cards during a hand so they don't accidentally get pushed into the muck in the middle of the table. It was one of the ZZ Top key chains from all the famous videos they made. When Sully busted Dusty he won the keychain as well. Lucky.

Then Sully busted one of the online players named Rob. Sully made a straight on the turn. Bye Rob. Sully was running good.

The tournament was five handed now. Over the next few hours I was quietly hanging around under the radar, picking my spots, my stack of chips steadily growing. Then this key hand happened.

I'm going to use a bit more shorthand—it's not too difficult to follow.

FYI:

s = spade, c = club, d = diamond, h = heart, A = ace,
K = king, Q = queen, J = jack, os = off suit

Blinds: The blinds are forced bets posted by players to the
left of the dealer button in flop-style poker games. The player
to the left of the dealer button places the small blind and the
big blind is then posted by the next player to the left.

Ante: a forced bet in which all players put an equal amount of
money or chips into the pot before the deal begins.

Button: the dealer button is a marker used to indicate the
player who is dealing or in casino games with a house dealer,
the player who acts last on that deal (who would be the dealer
in a home game).

The blinds were $500/$1,000 with a $100 ante. I have 810c in
the big blind. Online guy Ian has Ad3h and goes all-in with his
last $200. Sully calls with Ah7c. I check. Sully says, "Ya wanna
check it down?" The flop comes 7sJd10s. The action is on me, and
I bet $2,000. Sully calls. The 6h comes on the turn. Sully checks.
Phil Hellmuth says, "Sully wants to check it down to get rid of a
player." I didn't know what *check it down* meant. It means Sully
and I would agree to not bet, just check all the way to the end of
the hand, and then we all turn over our cards to see who won, usually ending with the all-in player getting knocked out. I bet $2,000
again. Phil says, "I like Scott's bet. He flopped middle pair with a
straight draw, and he has the best hand." Sully is staring at me with
a curious half-smile, trying to read my face, looking for info, and
says, "Look at me. Do you know I have the ZZ Top keychain?" as he
dangles it in front of my face. I smiled back at him, revealing nothing, only saying, "Yeah, I want it." Phil, commenting on the action,

says, "Sully wants to check it down and get rid of a player, but Scott's doing the right thing." Finally Sully folds to my bet. Online guy Ian needs an ace on the river to make a pair and beat my pair of tens. There are only two aces left in the deck. "He's a twenty-to-one underdog. There are forty winning cards for Scott and only two for Ian," Phil notes. The jack of hearts comes on the river, and I take it down. I won a big pot, and I'm now the chip leader. More importantly I learned that if I got aggressive with Sully, it messed with his game. It seemed like he didn't think I could play aggressively. So I bust online player Ian, and there are now only four of us left. I have $44,400 in chips, Sully has $16,400, Ace has $15,600, and the remaining online player, Steve, has $3,600.

My goal then was to make it to the end no matter what, even if I had one chip and a chair, as they say. Now I was the chip leader. Could I hold on to my stack as well as I was able to rebuild my short stack? A few hands after I took the lead I got involved in a hand with Sully and online player Steve.

The blinds were $600/$1,200 with a $100 ante. Online player Steve limps in, Sully with A9os calls, and I check in the big blind with J2os. The flop comes AhJdAd. Sully checks his set (three-of-a-kind, remember?). I check. Online player Steve goes all-in for his last $2,200. Sully bets $6,000 like he should, trying to get me to fold so he's only up against online player Steve. That's a tactic I learned months after this game. Not knowing what to do and thinking my two pairs were good, I raise $12,000. Somewhere in my brain I was thinking Sully was trying to bluff me, acting like he had an ace in his hand. The pot had suddenly blown up to over $24,000. I should've folded to Sully's raise; I only had my big blind of $1,200 in the pot, and I could have walked away virtually unscathed. Nope. Sully goes all-in, $32,600 in the pot now. Sully tells me, "If you have the other ace, you win." Now I have over $13,000 in the pot, and it's only another $6,000 to $7,000 to call Sully's all-in. I was reeling. Was Sully bluffing? Or maybe I do have the best hand. I had to make a decision, and because I am not Charles Xavier, I called. Online player Steve guy had a diamond flush and tripled up. Sully won the big side pot. I lose, and just like that, Sully takes the chip lead.

Can you feel my stress level? I have zero poker knowledge to be able to make the decisions I am being tested with. I am not used to being in a situation where I have nothing to fall back on to help me get through, and suddenly I'm really feeling out of my element. Having the chip lead made me want to win. Before that I was just trying not to be the first guy out. The competitive dude in my brain suddenly woke up. I had tasted blood and wanted more.

The next hand blinds are still $600/$1,200 with a $100 ante. Online player Steve limps with pocket twos. I call with 6h9h. Ace checks his big blind with 10d5s. The flop is 2c5h6s. I have top pair. There's $4,400 in the pot. I check. Ace checks. Online player Steve bets $1,500. I call. Ace calls. Now the pot is $8,900. The turn card is the 4c. I check. Ace checks. Online player Steve bets $4,000, and not knowing what to do, I say in desperation, "What do I do, Phil?" I can't hear Phil explaining, "Scott should fold. If he had played another week or two of poker in his life, he'd be able to fold top pair, but being an amateur in this spot makes it very hard to do." He's right about that. Phil continues, "Look at Scott. He is sensing something about the hand, and he wants to fold, but I can't blame him for calling. Look at the process he's going through. He even made the comment that 'If I lose this pot, I won't have enough chips to play Sully heads up for the title.' He's in a tough spot."

I called the $4,000. I couldn't fold it. The pot is now up to $16,900. Ace calls; he should've folded as well. The pot is $20,900. The river card is the Kh. I check, and Ace goes all-in! "Bad time to bluff, Ace," Phil says as Ace's pair of fives are no match for online player Steve's set of twos. It's $5,600 for me to call, and now

I fold. Phil says, "Good lay down" about my fold. Online player Steve wins the hand, and Ace is decimated. I just lost 30 percent of my chips, and I'm now down to just ten big blinds, my recent glory of being chip leader now a distant memory as I struggle to keep it together. I decided I would just keep my head down for a few hands, really tighten up, and only play really premium hands, QQ, KK, and AA. The cards made my decisions easy for a few hands: I was dealt nothing but crap and was able to calm down. I realized that any remnants of not sleeping or being drunk from the night before were gone. The five or six Bloody Marys I put down may as well have been virgins. I was truly adrenalized on poker.

The blinds were up to $800/$1,600 with a $200 ante. I was getting close to shove-or-fold territory again, and then I caught a break. Ace was all-in for his last $700 with 10d4s. Online player Steve calls with Q10s. Sully raises $4,500 with AA. I can't fold fast enough. Insta-fold. Online player Steve calls. I'm hoping Sully busts both of them. The flop is 9s3d7s. Sully bets $10,000—go Sully! Steve has a spade flush draw, and he goes all-in. Sully insta-calls—there's $67,100 in the pot! I say, "Thankfully I have no part of this!" The turn card is the Kc, and the 3c comes on the river. Online player Steve bricks, and Sully's aces hold and he busts both of them.

And just like that, it was down to two.

Sully takes two. Courtesy Lisa Tenner.

I did it! Somehow I had outlasted everyone else, playing so very carefully that I was able to navigate the tournament to the final level. I was heads-up with Sully, the best player in the tournament. Granted, I was in bad shape chip-wise. Of the $80,000 in chips in play, Sully had $65,000; I had $15,000. He had an over four-to-one chip advantage, and the odds were heavily, crushingly, monumentally, overwhelmingly—is that enough adverbs? I think not, so here's one more—brutally in his favor. Even I didn't think I could win. No one did. I could hear Antonio and Phil talking with Phil Hellmuth (I didn't even really know who he was yet, just that he was a big deal), and they were saying how Sully had me crushed and there was no way I could beat him with him holding such an advantage over me in chips and experience. Sully was a seasoned player, I was the definition of rank amateur, and the pros had already written me off, the outcome a foregone conclusion.

Man, were they in for a shock.

Our tournament director, Matt Savage, repositioned me and Sully at the table for heads-up play. We had been sitting next to each other the whole tournament, talking a lot, busting balls. Now we were at either end of the table, across from the dealer, ready to do battle to the death—or until one of us had all the chips. Okay, here we go.

Here's the poker glossary for you again so you have it right in front of you:

s = spade, **c** = club, **d** = diamond, **h** = heart, **A** = ace, **K** = king, **Q** = queen, **J** = jack, **os** = off suit

Blinds: The blinds are forced bets posted by players to the left of the dealer button in flop-style poker games. The player to the left of the dealer button places the small blind and the big blind is then posted by the next player to the left.

Ante: a forced bet in which all players put an equal amount of money or chips into the pot before the deal begins.

Button: the dealer button is a marker used to indicate the player who is dealing or in casino games with a house dealer, the player who acts last on that deal (who would be the dealer in a home game).

Heads-up for the championship! Here are the decisive hands as they went down.

The blinds were $1,000/$2,000 with a $300 ante. Sully just calls with Qh2s. I check 10s3s. The flop is 7dQs6s. Sully has top pair, and I have a flush draw. I bet $4,000, which is almost as much as there is in the pot. I was trying to be aggressive and bet big to get him to fold his hand. Phil says, "Scott doesn't have many chips left, only seven big blinds. I can see them getting all-in here." Mark Tenner says, "This is Sully's tournament to lose." Phil comments, "Sully has top pair, and he pretty much knows he has the best hand, so if he doesn't move it all-in here, it's only because he's trying to trap Scott for the rest of his chips." Sully calls the $4,000. The turn card is the 4c. Now I have a straight draw and a flush draw. I bet $3,000. The right move would be to go all-in at this point, but I was scratching and clawing, trying to hold onto enough chips to play one more hand. It was so intense in the moment, and even later watching the TV broadcast and knowing the outcome I feel nervous watching myself! Sully says, "I'll put ya' all-in," which means if I call him, it would put me all-in and my tournament life at risk. "Yeah, let's go for it!" I yell. There's $27,600 in the pot. Sully is a three-to-one favorite to win the hand and take the title. I need a spade!!! The dealer deals the river card, and it is the 8s, and I make my flush and pump both fists in the air exclaiming, "YEAHHHHHH!" Phil exclaimed, "Scott has doubled up and is back in it! Scott is back, baby!"

Nailed it! Love that river card.
Left to right: Sully, tournament director extraordinaire Matt Savage, and me, doing my best Ben Grimm, "IT'S CLOBBERIN' TIME!" Courtesy Lisa Tenner.

Chip count: Sully $48,200. Me $31,800.
Courtesy Lisa Tenner.

We play a bunch of quick hands; Sully raises and I fold. I raise and Sully folds. I have an ace the last two hands I raise. Amazingly I'm dealt Ad3d, three aces in a row heads-up. I'm really catching cards. This time I just call after raising the last two and getting no action from Sully. Sully checks in the big blind with 7h4c. The flop comes Ah5d7s. Wow. I pair my ace. Do you know how hard it is to make a pair on the flop in poker? It's hard. Phil chimes in, "It looks to me like it's going to work out pretty well for Scott because he's flopped top pair and Sully has flopped second pair. They're playing one-on-one poker now, and second pair is a pretty strong hand,

and I have a feeling Sully can get himself in trouble now unless he hits a seven or a four."

Running good. Courtesy Lisa Tenner.

Sully acts first and checks. I bet $5,000. Sully puts his head down in what looks like frustration. Mark Tenner comments, "Sully is a little bit down. The hands have not been going his way." Sully takes a minute, maybe he's thinking I am making a move on him, and then he check-raises $15,000 with his pair of sevens. Phil comments, "And Sully is going to make the raise. I like the raise. Of course if he could see Scott's hand Sully could fold his hand but he doesn't know what Scott has. He's made a nice raise here. It's a good play." It's $10,000 more for me to call. I think my pair of aces are good. I'm not thinking that he could also have an ace with a better kicker, meaning a card higher than a three. Phil says, "Scott should've put all his money in right there. If he's calling $10,000, he should shove all-in now." Of course that would be the right move, but I just call the $10,000. Phil says, "There's a lot of inexperience here. Scott hasn't played much poker before, but he's really picking this game up on the fly. You really have to give him credit." The turn card is the Jd. Now I have top pair and a diamond flush draw. Sully checks. Again, I don't know that all-in is the right move—Phil and Mark are practically yelling at me to put all my money in! I only bet $4,000. Sully calls. There's $42,600 in the pot. The Jc comes on the river.

Sully checks and I check! SO BAD. I should've bet the river, but I was so paranoid about losing chips that I was playing way too safe. What if he had AJ? I take down a nice pot, but I should've gotten more. I'm the chip leader now. Phil says, "That was a key pot right there, and the fact that Scott just called with an ace before the flop threw Sully off and cost him an extra $19,000." It's not like I made some premeditated move; I didn't know I was supposed to raise. As Bob Ross would say, "There are no mistakes, just happy accidents."

Chip count: Me $61,200. Sully $18,800. Courtesy Lisa Tenner.

I can tell Sully is starting to crack. He's talking a lot, complaining about his cards. Mark Tenner says, "Phil, your protégé is whining just like you!" Phil replied, "Are you saying I whine too much at the table?" "Yes, you're the Poker Brat," Mark answered. Phil said, "Ya got me! What can I say? I wouldn't be much of a man if I didn't admit to my faults." I learned later that Phil Hellmuth's nickname was the Poker Brat because of the tantrums he'd throw at the table when he didn't like the way a hand played out or how the game was going. He was very passionate! I just kept my cool and commiserated with Sully. I wasn't going to kick him while he was down. I'm not a shit-talker ever when it comes to sports or competing. That karma will always come back and get ya.

The heads-up play continues; the blinds have gone up to $1,200/ $2,400 with a $400 ante. I look down at A3 again! Just like the last hand except this time it's spades. Another ace! Unbelievable. I just call again. That seems to be working for me. Sully checks his 10s3c. The flop is 7d7hJd. Sully says, "I'll bet that." He bets $4,000. Mark Tenner says, "He's on a stone-cold bluff." I call. Phil says, "Here's the problem with playing against an amateur: Sully made a nice bet there, a stone-cold bluff actually, and Scott called him with ace high right away. Ace high is just not that strong of a hand, but then again, Scott was right." Sully said, "You always get a piece of that flop, don't ya?" I just shrugged, playing it cool, and started to realize that he's off his game; he doesn't know how to play against whatever it is I am doing, so I'll just keep doing it. Turn is the 6d, Sully checks, and Mark comments, "Sully couldn't fire the second bullet." Meaning he didn't want to bet again and continue trying to bluff me. I bet $4,000, what Phil calls "a semi-bluff," and Sully folds. Phil says, "And Sully can't believe it. He's thinking Scott can't always have a hand. Well, guess what?" Mark says, "Scott is now controlling this game for sure, and with Lady Luck on his side, he has taken a commanding lead."

Chip count: Me $68,600. Sully $11,400. Courtesy Lisa Tenner.

Mark comments, "Scott knows how Sully felt just a little while ago. Sully needs some of that Scott Ian luck. He needs to win three hands in a row, big confrontations to win this tournament."

The cards are out on the next hand, and I look down at Ac8d. A8—the dead man's hand! According to legend it's the hand Wild Bill Hickock was holding when he was shot to death in the middle of a game. I've always loved numbers like thirteen that are considered bad luck so to me, the A8 is a good omen. And just a quick flash-forward: it'll only be a little over two years from this moment that I'd be opening a bar called Dead Man's Hand in Las Vegas with Jerry Cantrell from Alice in Chains.

Back to the hand. I am first to act, and I just call again. Phil says, "Scott limps with an ace again! He keeps limping with an ace he should be raising!" Sully immediately goes all-in with Qs5s. I call! I could see the look on Sully's face when I instantly call: he's not happy. I'm sure he was hoping to shove and have me fold. Now I have Sully on the hook: all of his chips are in the middle, and his tournament life is on the line. Mark says, "This is the big one. If the best starting hand wins, Scott wins." Sully says, "It's not pretty," commenting on his queen-high hand against my ace. Sully and I are both standing up, waiting for the flop to be dealt. Phil says, "Scott looks like a boxer out there!" I was jumping up and down like I was skipping rope at boxing training, trying to stay loose and not throw up from nerves! The flop is Kc8s4c. I pair my eight, and I've only got to fade (avoid) a queen (only three left) or Sully making runner-runner (two in a row) spades for a flush.

The heads-up all-in flop. Courtesy Lisa Tenner.

Sully is dancing, doing what I think is called the running-man and yelling at the poker gods for a queen. I've got my hands on top of my head and am saying *ace ace ace ace ace ace* in my brain.

Ace ace ace ace ace ace. . . . Courtesy Lisa Tenner.

The turn card is the 7c. Now Sully only has three outs. Only a queen on the river can save him.

The 7c on the turn. Courtesy Lisa Tenner.

Time seemed to slow down waiting for the dealer to deal the final card.

My brain was a tornado inside my skull; every muscle in my body was tensed like I was about to get in a fight. I was holding my breath in anticipation of the last card, and then the river is dealt and it's the 8h, and it's over. I punched my fist hard into the air, all the tension leaving my body in a scream from my gut, "YEAH-HHHHHHH!" And then again with both fists pumping, "YEAHH-HHHHHHH!" I was so excited, the Joker-like smile on my face so wide that it could lop off the rest of my head above it. I had done something I thought was completely impossible, literally for me a miracle. I was stunned. I just stood there taking it all in. Everyone was cheering and backslapping me and trying to talk to me, and all I wanted to do was kiss and hug Pearl like Rocky looking for Adrian at the end of *Rocky*. Mark Tenner said, "The fighter beat the dancer Phil. Once again Lady Luck smiled down on Scott Ian. He had the best cards, and they held up." Phil and Mark came down to the table from where they were commentating, and I shook hands with them and with Phil Laak and Antonio. I remember looking at Pearl in the audience; we both had the same giant smiles on our faces.

The thrill of victory. Courtesy Lisa Tenner.

And the agony of defeat.
There's that Joker smile. Courtesy Lisa Tenner.

Sully was talking to Phil, telling him, "I couldn't catch a hand—eight, nine hands in a row it was seven-three, nine-deuce, eight-four. I was just waiting for a face card, and I saw one, and I freaked out, and I pushed all-in. He decapitated me, man. I just had a really bad run at the end."

He's not lying. He really did have a bad run, and I had a great run.

Sully continued, "My plan worked. I wanted to get to heads-up and then hopefully face someone inexperienced."

Phil Laak said, "If he didn't keep waking up with cards, you would've taken it. But he kept waking up."

Looking back on it now I can pinpoint a couple of things that happened heads-up against Sully. I had nothing to lose and was playing that way, with zero fear. I never should've lasted in the game as long as I did, so I was just happy to be there and was having fun. And then on top of that, even a novice like me knew what to do with the run of cards I got dealt heads-up. With each hand I won, my confidence grew. Sully and I were conversing back and forth, and he was giving me info just by talking with me. I could tell he was confused by my play as I had played very safe the whole game and now all of a sudden I was being aggressive. He didn't know whether I was bluffing or if I really had a hand. He didn't know if I even knew how to bluff (I understood the concept of bluffing but had never actually tried it). My read on him at that point was that he was overthinking what was happening and that I would take advantage of that. To understate a poker phrase, I was running good. I was on a heater, as they say, and everything was going my way. I had won five hands in a row, and Sully was reeling and on the ropes. I came back from insurmountable odds, almost a five-to-one chip deficit all the way to being up six-to-one in chips and about to deliver the knockout punch to kill the giant. The dead man's hand took care of that, and I was the winner.

Phil gave me my trophy, which was very cool. More importantly they handed me one of those giant checks made out for $25,000 to the charity I was playing for, LIFEbeat.

L-R: Vinnie, Ace, Antonio Esfandiari, your boy,
Phil Hellmuth, Sully, Phil Laak, and Dusty.

Courtesy Lisa Tenner.

Anyone have a giant FedEx envelope? Courtesy Lisa Tenner.

After all the handshaking and good-byes Phil Hellmuth came over and asked me how often I played poker. I told him I had never played no-limit hold 'em in my life before this tournament. He laughed and said he could tell because my game was a mess but my instincts were good and I had a lot of patience. He told me that my patience was the reason I won the tournament and that patience was something you could not teach. Phil gave me his phone number and told me that if I ever wanted to learn more about poker to give him a call. I thanked him and just nodded and smiled a lot. I really didn't know what he was talking about and just wanted to go eat and take a nap. Remember, I didn't even know who Phil was at the time; I just knew he was some poker pro. It wasn't until I got home from the trip and Googled him that I found out he was the Michael Jordan of poker. I thought it was interesting that this (at the time) nine-time World Series of Poker bracelet winner took a minute to tell me that if I ever wanted to get serious, to give him a call.

A week later I had forgotten all about it. Poker had disappeared from my radar. Or so I thought . . .

To be continued in All-In, Part Two, later on in this book.

THE LAND OF
RAPE & S.O.D.

If it weren't for my guitar riffs and monster tone on S.O.D.'s *Speak English or Die*, Trent Reznor wouldn't have won an Oscar.

Yep, I just wrote that. And I'd guess that right about now you're thinking, *Is he fucking high?*

Nope. I'm allergic.

Let me explain . . .

I met Al Jourgensen, the man behind seminal industrial band Ministry, in the early nineties, and we immediately hit it off. It was a fuck-fest of mutual respect. Ministry was about to head out on the 1992 Lollapalooza tour, and Al invited me to their shows in New York and asked if I wanted to get up and play with them. I was a big Ministry fan. S.O.D. covered the Ministry songs "Thieves" and "Stigmata" to fill out our set on tour. I'd seen Ministry live a bunch of times, so to get on stage and be a part of that Dante's Inferno of a rock show was something I had to do. The first night of their three-night stint at the Jones Beach amphitheater I played on one song, a cover of Black Sabbath's "Supernaut," and when it was over all I could think was, *I need more of that.* I felt like I was playing on the edge of a cliff, and falling off was the fun part.

I guess I passed the audition because the next night I played two songs with them, on the third show at Jones Beach I was up there for four, and by the time the Los Angeles shows rolled around a few weeks later I was on stage playing half the set, including some of their best songs like "Burning Inside," "Just One

Fix," "So What," "Thieves," "Stigmata," and "N.W.O." It was a fucking nerve-shattering blast, and Al would hand his guitar over to me, freeing him up to create even more onstage chaos than usual. I had the responsibility of playing all his parts, and his guitar was loud as fuck, in the monitors on stage and out front to the audience, as loud as a jet engine. There was no way to hide in the mix, and if I made a mistake, everyone would hear it. In a normal band situation this wouldn't be a problem for me—I'm not going to cause a train wreck—but this was Ministry, and there was Al riding around the stage on a mic stand made out of animal bones and cow skulls, crashing into anything and anyone. There was real physical danger, and there was no safe word—you just had to play like your life was at risk, because it was. It was true anarchy, and I had never been a part of something so crazy. I liked it. A lot.

Wait, so how does this have anything to do with Trent and his Oscar?

Patience, my friends, patience.

Trent Reznor started out in Cleveland in the mid-eighties playing in pop bands. Then he discovered Ministry and started writing heavier electronic songs with an edgier and dance-ier sound that would become the template for NIN. Before he recorded anything that anyone heard he actually worked as a roadie for Ministry, which was like getting shipped off to boot camp and pledge-hazing week at the frat house all in one. Not only did he learn about killer guitar tones and extreme onstage battle royals; he also learned how to dodge lit firecrackers and deflect flying beer bottles. One night Al mickied him and shaved his head and eyebrows. But Trent didn't flinch and returned from the ordeal undaunted, enraged, and stronger for it. He wrote and recorded his breakthrough album *Pretty Hate Machine* in 1989 and then the metallic Ministry-esque *Broken* in 1992. The rest is history.

A year later, the summer of 1993, Anthrax released *Sound of White Noise*. Al did remixes of two of the songs, "Potter's Field" and "Hy Pro Glo." We headed out on a US tour to support the record with White Zombie and Quicksand opening for us. It was a killer package. White Zombie's song "Thunder Kiss '65" had become pretty much the main theme of MTV's animated hit series *Beavis and Butt-Head,* and they were on the verge of blowing up. Al came to the show in Chicago, and after the show we headed out in his brand-new Nissan 300ZX; at the time it was one of the fastest cars you could buy. We were speeding through downtown Chicago at 110 mph, jumping median strips, going the wrong way on one-way streets, and somehow not dying.

And now we *flashback to the summer of 1992 . . .*

The Lollapalooza tour had just played Chicago. Al and Eddie Vedder are out postshow, tearing through the streets of Chicago in another barely street-legal car that Al shouldn't be driving. All the while there's eardrum-shattering music cranked on Al's car stereo as Eddie holds on for his life, Al turning downtown Chicago into his own private Grand Prix. Eddie can't help but listen to the music—it's so loud you can't not listen—and all he knows is it's the heaviest thing he's ever heard in his life and seems to be playing on a loop. Time speeds by, and eventually Al screeches to a halt in front of Eddie's hotel, and it's a miracle in itself that anyone even remembered where the hotel was. Eddie happily says goodnight to his maniacal chauffeur, and as he's getting out of the car Al pops the tape out of the player and hands it to Eddie: "This is for you to remember this night by. S.O.D. *Speak English or Die*." Eddie takes the tape and stands there dazed as Al peels out into the early morning Chicago heat.

Okay, nice anecdote about Eddie, but what does that have to do with Trent?

Wait for it . . .

A year later in the summer of 1993 . . .

So we're flying around Chicago in Al's Japanese rocket, and Al has the S.O.D. tape cranked and is singing and playing air guitar at me. I'm smiling big on the outside but on the inside all I can think is what bad luck it would be to die while listening to "The Ballad of Jimi Hendrix." By the way, for the "Ballad of Scott Ian," just use the "March of the S.O.D." intro riff two times: duh duh, chucka, duh duh, chucka, duh duh chucka duh duh, you're dead. It's in my will to have that played at my funeral.

Al lands the rocket outside some bar, and before we get out of the car he tells me—very nonchalantly, I might add—that S.O.D. is the reason he wanted to put heavy guitars into Ministry's music and change from being a synthy new wave band into the industrial juggernaut the world knows them as today. That back in the eighties he heard S.O.D., and that was the influence, the impetus to become the Ministry that would make *The Land of Rape and Honey, The Mind Is a Terrible Thing to Taste, In Case You Didn't Feel Like Showing Up,* and the rest. I couldn't believe it, and in my drunken/terrified state I figured he was joking. But he wasn't.

My mind reeled at the thought, trying to make sense out of it. S.O.D. covered Ministry, I played with Ministry, and the whole time it had been a direct result of something I did back in 1985. Somehow S.O.D. was responsible for Ministry and everything they influenced. It was like the movie *Looper* without the hitmen. Well, okay, maybe not wholly responsible for Ministry and everything they influenced, but at least partially, and that's where I get off saying Trent wouldn't have won an Oscar for scoring the Facebook movie *The Social Network*, nor would NIN even exist.

HA! Take that, nineties!!!

I kid, of course. After all, it is an honor.

And Trent rules.

I have another story about Al that is worth telling even though Al tells it in his memoir *Ministry: The Lost Gospels of Al Jourgensen* as well. The difference is that I have the corroborating story from Steven Spielberg. Yes, that Steven Spielberg.

In 2000 Spielberg approached Ministry to play a band in a scene in his movie *A.I. Artificial Intelligence*. Yes, I know the movie sucked, but I'm not here to review it, and I apologize for reminding you of something so terrible. Still, Al didn't know that many would consider the movie to be Spielberg's worst; it would be huge exposure, and they were getting paid well to do it. And it's fucking Steven Spielberg.

So Ministry flew to Los Angeles to shoot their scene. They'd been on set a few hours, just hanging out in their trailer in a typical hurry-up-and-wait scenario, and suddenly there was a knock on the door.

An assistant of Steven's told them that Mr. Spielberg was on his way to meet the band. Al told me he was as excited as anyone else to meet Spielberg but wanted to think of something special to say. He didn't want to be on the end of some lame receiving line and to just shake hands and say, "Hi, nice to meet you." That's not Al's style.

Spielberg shows up at Ministry's trailer with his entourage of assistants and basically glad-hands his way down the line, saying, "Hello, and thanks for being in my movie" to all the band members.

Al is last, and as Spielberg shakes his hand, Al grabs it in a vice grip and shakes it extra hard, and as Spielberg reiterates the same bland greeting to Al, Al replies, "Yeah Steve, I need to talk to you about your movie."

The simultaneous intake of breath from all of Spielberg's assistants was as loud as a Ministry show, followed quickly by an awkward silence, everyone in the room frozen in that moment, staring at Al and Steven Spielberg.

Al, thriving in the silent chaos he has created, continued to shake Spielberg's hand in his vice grip. Spielberg slowly waking out of his scripted behavior, confused and taken aback that someone is even talking to him, finally asks, "What about my movie?"

Al, still shaking Spielberg's hand and right up in Spielberg's face, immediately replies, "Steve, do we look like a band that would be in a movie about some robot kid and a talking teddy bear?"

Spielberg, now even more confused and annoyed, is looking around at his assistants for an answer, "Did he get a script? Did you send him the script?" Looking back at Al, "Didn't you read the script?"

Al interrupts Spielberg's questioning, "Steve! Do we look like we want to be in a movie about some fucking robot kid and a goddamn fucking talking teddy bear? We're fucking Ministry! We were told this movie was called *A.I. Anal Intruder!*"

Spielberg is blown away, freaking out. No one ever speaks to him like this, and he's looking at his people in disbelief as he stammers back at Al, "Who told you this? Who told you it was called *Anal Intruder?*"

Al waits a beat, waits another beat, making Spielberg sweat, and then he claps him on the shoulder and says, "Aww Steve, I'm just fucking with ya!"

Spielberg is silent. No one in the room dares make a sound, and then after what seems like an eternity Spielberg starts to laugh. All his assistants follow suit, of course, suddenly relieved that the king isn't going to have their collective heads. Spielberg slowly walks out of the room laughing and telling Al, "You're a funny guy, Al, very funny . . ."

Spielberg and his entourage leave, and Al figured they'd be thrown off the set, fired immediately, go-directly-to-jail-do-not-pass-go FIRED.

A few hours slowly pass, and there's another knock on the door. It was one of the assistants summoning Mr. Jourgensen to the set to see Mr. Spielberg. *So this was it*, Al thought, *we're done. Well*, he thought, *at least he's got the balls to tell me to my face.* As Al was escorted onto the set, into Spielberg's director's world, he noticed a chair with his name across the back right next to Spielberg's director's chair. *What the hell?* Al thought as Spielberg, all smiles and hand-shakey, proudly showed Al the chair he had made for him and had set up next to his so Al could watch the shoot the same way he did, telling Al if there's anything he needs, to just ask. Apparently Al's way of breaking the ice had worked, and now he was Spielberg's best friend, with Spielberg even buying Al a really expensive leather duster jacket and treating Ministry like gold for the rest of the week they were there shooting.

Cut to January 2003, and I am in Germany promoting Anthrax's album *We've Come for You All*. I had finished my promo trip in Germany at the same time my then-girlfriend (now wife), Pearl, was in Stuttgart to perform with her dad's band on a German TV show called *Wetten Das*, which was like a three-hour-long *Tonight Show* that only aired six or seven times a year. It was the biggest Saturday night TV show in Germany, maybe even all of Europe, so they would get the biggest celebrities promoting whatever new movie/record/book they had coming out. I was having a who-the-hell-let-me-in-here moment hanging out backstage with Steven Spielberg, Tom Hanks, Leonardo DiCaprio, Meat Loaf, Hugh Grant, Faith Hill, and Christina Aguilera.

So it's this big celebrity soiree backstage, with everybody talking to everybody except for Christina Aguilera, who apparently was so extra famous and important that she needed her own dressing room in a separate hall guarded by giants who looked like they would later appear in *Game of Thrones*. Good for her.

Spielberg, Hanks, and DiCaprio, those three kind-of-but-not-as-famous-as Christina Aguilera stars, were there promoting their new movie, *Catch Me If You Can*.

As a rule, I normally never approach anyone, but Spielberg and I had a mutual friend in Al, and I had to ask him about *Anal Intruder*. But I wasn't going to just drop the *Anal Intruder* thing on him, because that'd be rude. I had to finesse this, so I came up with an icebreaker: Spielberg's mother owned a restaurant right near my house in LA, and of course he'd want to talk about that, right?

Spielberg was talking to DiCaprio, and when their conversation ended he was standing by himself. I walked over and introduced myself and told him I really liked his mom's restaurant and that it's right down the street from my house. At first he didn't reply, looking past me, not paying any attention. I started to turn to walk away, I wasn't going to push it, but then he looked at me and said, "Wait, what did you just say about my mother?" I repeated myself, and a big smile spread across his face, very excited and proud to talk about his mom's restaurant. We had a nice conversation, and at some point he asked me what I was doing there. I explained that I was there with my lady and that she sang with Meat Loaf. He told me he was excited to see Meat perform and then asked me what I did. I told him I played in a heavy metal band called Anthrax. He told me he had heard of us, though he hadn't actually heard our music, but he did know the name, and then he said to me

STEVE: I know someone in a heavy metal band.
ME: [playing dumb] Oh really?
STEVE: Yes, Al Jourgensen from Ministry. Do you know him?
ME: EE-Yeeeeeesss! [sounding like Frank Nelson from the *Jack Benny* show—Google it]
STEVE: Oh great!

And then Steve leans in a bit toward me and looks around the room like he's about to tell a racist joke and says

STEVE: Do you know he thought my *A.I.* movie was a porn called *Anal Intruder*?

ME: [playing dumb again] No, you're kidding! That's hilarious!

We were both laughing, and he told me to please say hello to Al for him and that next time I was at his mom's restaurant to tell her that we met and to say hello to her as well.

I walked off, thinking how the man who gave us *E.T.* and *Schindler's List* had just said "Anal Intruder" and "say hello to my mom" in practically the same sentence.

You're welcome.

BEWARE THE LESHY

Once upon a time three friends named Scott, Whitfield, and Robert went on a snowboarding adventure to the greatest of all mountains, Whistleblack Mountain. The tallest, biggest, snowiest, and, some would even say, magicalest mountain in the world.

Scott, Whitfield, and Robert were so excited to be together in this incredible place riding their snowboards and having an awesome time. They rode and rode and rode down every trail the mountain had to offer and then back up to the top on the gondola and then down again, racing each other and laughing all the while.

The only thing missing from this perfect day was powder, that light and fluffy snow that made you feel like you were floating. But even without powder they were having fun and kept an eye out for that wonderful kind of snow.

After an especially long ride the three friends decided to ride the gondola and take a break at the top of the mountain. It was a beautiful day. Not a cloud in the sky. The three friends each ordered a hot chocolate with whipped cream—yum!—to warm up their bellies, and they sat outside in the winter sun, drinking them and laughing about all the fun they were having.

Hot chocolates finished, they were walking to where they left their boards when Scott noticed a sign a little ways down a path from where they were. The sign read: DANGER! OFF PISTE (which means snowboarding that is done on areas of snow that have not been specially prepared for riding on) BEYOND THIS POINT YOU RIDE AT YOUR OWN RISK! And below that in smaller, messier writing: BEWARE THE LE

Scott said to Robert and Whitfield, "Hey guys, look at that sign. I know it says DANGER! But maybe there's powder in the woods behind it?"

"Yeah, maybe there is, but what do you think BEWARE THE LE means?" Whitfield asked. The three friends could see that LE was just the beginning of another word, but the rest of the word was covered with ice and snow. "Maybe it means there's a ledge or something like a cliff?" Robert answered. They all agreed that's probably what it meant.

The three friends were very excited about the possibility of powder, so they strapped into their boards and rode over to the sign.

The sign was old, very old—painted letters fading and the wood was cracked and it was hanging crookedly from a tall wooden post. It looked like it had been there for a really long time. Behind the sign was a deep, dark forest packed with the tallest trees that went on and on as far as their eyes could see. Whitfield was staring into the trees and exclaimed, "The snow looks really deep in there! I think it's powder!"

"It is!" cried Scott.

"Yeahhhhh, let's do it!" yelled Robert, and the three friends rode beyond the sign, Scott bumping it with his board as they passed.

None of them noticed the ice and snow that fell from the sign revealing the rest of its warning:

BEWARE THE LESHY

Scott, Whitfield, and Robert were ecstatic. The snow in the forest was the lightest, fluffiest, deepest untouched powder any of them had ever encountered. They were flying through the trees, floating on the snowy air cushion the powder created for their boards. Never had any of them experienced such perfect conditions. The snow was so pristine that it was like no one had ever ridden in the forest before the three friends discovered it.

Because no one had for a very long time.

If the warning sign wasn't enough to scare people off, the rumors and stories about people entering the forest to ride the perfect snow and never being seen again certainly kept people away. But these were all local legends, and Scott, Whitfield, and Robert were from far, far away. They didn't know that the forest on Whistleblack Mountain was the domain of the Leshy, an evil forest fairy that can assume any likeness, shape-shifting into any form, animal or man, and it likes nothing more than tricking stray travelers into entering its forest—or worse.

As soon as the three friends crossed behind the sign into the forest the Leshy, sleeping in its cave, awoke. It knew there were intruders because the trees whispered to him right away so as not to incur the wrath of the Leshy. There was a time when the trees would keep quiet if someone accidentally entered the forest, not wanting some poor soul to be tricked by the Leshy—or worse. But when the Leshy found out the trees were allowing strangers into the forest he told the trees in his deep rumbly voice, "Trees, this is my forest, and let it be not poisoned by those who do not belong within. I demand ye reveal to me the very moment the sanctity of my ground is fouled. If ye do not, I shall pull and twist your branches until they are broken off and burn your wood to warm my cave—or worse." And so the trees listened. And they told.

The Leshy was not happy about being woken up as it was enjoying its winter hibernation. It had been a very long time since someone had dared enter the forest. Most people obeyed the sign. But Scott, Whitfield, and Robert weren't most people.

They were heavy metal dudes.

Scott played in a band called Anthrax, Whitfield in a band called Ugly Kid Joe, and Robert, well, he played in the biggest band in the land: Metallica. The three of them were always going on adventures all over the world. They were fearless warriors looking to have the most fun they could have, even if it meant sometimes bending a rule, like disobeying a warning sign. The three of them were riding all over through the trees, going as fast as they could, and at some point Scott and Whitfield became separated from Robert. This was okay though: they'd either see each other on the way down or would meet up when they got to the bottom.

The Leshy left its cave and quickly found the trails that the three amigos were leaving behind in the deep, powdery snow. The Leshy shape-shifted into very long legs and big-clawed snowshoe size feet so he could move very easily and fast through the deep snow. It laughed at how easy they were making it to be tracked. They weren't even trying to cover their tracks, almost like they didn't even know it existed! The Leshy said to the trees, "Everyone knows of the Leshy and how I trick intruders in my forest by leading them astray—or worse. Right, my woody friends?" The trees quietly agreed. They didn't want the Leshy to pull their branches off and burn them. But under the ground where all the tree roots in the forest touched each other a feeling was growing. A feeling that they didn't want the Leshy to hurt the three humans who were only having fun and weren't hurting anyone. The trees were tired of the tyrannical Leshy and were not going to take its orders anymore. It was the right thing to do. The trees talked from root to root that they would do whatever they could to help the three friends and stop the Leshy.

And some of the trees even whispered, "Or worse."

About halfway down the mountain Scott and Whitfield snowboarded up to a giant rock among the trees. It was a boulder the size of a house right at the edge of a cliff. If you went the wrong way around the boulder, you'd fall all the way down to the bottom of the mountain. They decided to stop at the rock and take a break, as their legs were getting tired from riding in the deep snow. The two of them unstrapped from their boards and sat with their backs leaning against the rock, catching their breath. It was very quiet, the only sound the whispering of the wind through the trees. Scott and Whitfield weren't worried about Robert: he was an awesome snowboarder and would find his way down. They should've been worried.

They didn't know what was following him.

Scott and Whitfield strapped back into their snowboards and slowly made their way around the left side of the rock because as they were riding toward it earlier, they saw from above that this was the correct way; the left side was the way down through the forest and the right side was a cliff. They weren't sure whether Robert would see it, so, using pine needles, they made an arrow in the snow pointing the correct way and wrote, "GO THIS WAY." Satisfied that their friend would be okay, they rode around the rock, dropped back into the forest, and made their way down the mountain.

The Leshy came out of the trees and headed for the rock. It knew the forest better than anyone and knew they would stop at the rock. The Leshy saw the message they had left and decided to play a trick. An *Or Worse* trick. It kicked snow over the pine-needle arrow that Scott and Whitfield had left for Robert and made a new arrow pointing the wrong way around the rock. The Leshy knew that when Robert came upon this he'd think his friends left the message and would follow it right over the cliff, falling to his death. The Leshy smiled and growled, proud of this evil deception, and then crept back into the trees to wait for the doomed trespasser.

Robert came out of the trees from a different place from where Scott and Whitfield had come earlier. He hadn't seen that the right side of the rock was a cliff. He rode up to the rock, unstrapped one foot from his snowboard, and saw the pine needle message in the snow. *Ah, cool! Scott and Whitfield left me a note telling me which way to go,* he thought. Robert decided to take a minute to catch his breath like the other guys did, unknowing of the malevolent red eyes watching him from the forest, waiting for him to fall.

The trees knew this was the moment they needed to act. It was now or never.

One tree drove its roots up from beneath the snow and started to push the snow that the Leshy used to cover the real pine needle arrow off of it. Another tree lowered a branch and started to brush away the deceptive arrow. Robert saw the tree branch moving next to him and looked down to see what was happening. He couldn't believe what he was seeing. The tree branch had cleared away the Leshy's fake arrow and was pointing at the real arrow. Robert saw the arrow pointing in the right direction and was very confused. *How was this happening?* he worried. He thought, *Maybe it was the wind?* That seemed more believable than tree branches moving on their own with a purpose. Then the tree branch started pushing Robert in the right direction.

The Leshy saw all of this as well. Furious at the trees' betrayal, the Leshy charged out of the forest toward Robert roaring in anger! "YOU HAVE TRESPASSED IN THE FOREST OF THE LESHY!" he bellowed. "NOW YE WILL PAY!"

Robert beheld the Leshy, a giant man-like creature with what looked like buck's horns growing from all over its body. It had a face that looked like dark skin stretched too tightly over a long-snouted skull, with a mossy black beard hanging from its chin.

Its long-clawed fingers were reaching for Robert as the monster ran through the snow toward him screaming. Robert immediately started pushing away on his board as fast as he could, but the snow was too deep and his foot kept sinking. The Leshy was almost upon him, just about to grab him with its filthy claws when all of a sudden the ground exploded with tree roots shooting into the air between them, blocking the Leshy from his prey. "HOW DARE YOU CROSS ME, YE COWARDLY TIMBER? YOUR DIS-LOYALTY SHALL BE REWARDED!!!" The Leshy flailed at the roots encircling it, tearing at them and breaking them into pieces. But for every root it tore, another took its place. The Leshy was whirling in a circle, fighting the roots as they grabbed at it, pulling at its limbs, trying to tear it down.

Robert was amazed. He had stopped trying to get away and was watching, enchanted by this battle between the trees and the monster. As if sensing Robert's distraction, the trees grabbed at his legs with their roots and started to pull him away from the fray and around to the correct side of the rock to get him down the mountain and out of the forest to safety. The Leshy, refusing to be denied his prey, furiously battled the tree roots, mangling and severing every root in its path as it made its way toward Robert.

A whisper ran through the forest. The trees understood what needed to be done. They couldn't just stop the Leshy because the Leshy was relentless and would certainly exact a terrible vengeance on the trees for their betrayal. It was going to need to be an *Or Worse* solution if they were going to save the human.

All the branches from above the Leshy joined the fight. They were swinging at it, scratching and cutting it in a thousand places. The Leshy fought even harder, but now needing to defend itself from the roots *and* the branches, it was overwhelmed. Even with all its power, it was no match for the power of all the trees united as one against it. The branches grabbed the Leshy by the neck, arms, and legs, and they dragged the Leshy to the edge of the cliff at the side of the rock, holding it just over the precipice.

"Hahahahaha" the Leshy laughed. "So ye think a fall can kill me? Nothing can kill me in this forest, for its magic is me and I am it. Set me free to catch my escaping prey, ye craven thicket, and I will spare ye a most terrible reprisal. Drop me and let yon inter-loper escape, and I will destroy everything that lives in this forest and poison the land so nothing shall ever grow upon it for time everlasting." The Leshy finished speaking, and the only sound in all the forest was Robert's snowboard cutting through the snow; by now he had almost reached the bottom of the mountain.

The trees held the Leshy firm and the moment Robert left the forest they released the Leshy. The Leshy screamed its wrath and cursed the trees as it fell. Simultaneously as the trees released the Leshy they gathered all their strength, harnessing all their power into one mighty push and they sent the giant rock over the side of the cliff after the Leshy.

Robert burst out of the forest, riding faster than he ever had in his life. All the tree branches were pushing him down the hill and making sure he didn't fall. As soon as he was out of the forest he saw Scott and Whitfield standing and waiting for him in a clear-ing just outside the tree line. "RUN! GET OUT OF THERE NOW!" Robert yelled as loud as he could as he raced toward them, doing his best to save his friends like they had done for him when they left the message at the rock. Scott and Whitfield heard Robert yelling at them to move, so they did—and fast. The second they moved, the Leshy hit the ground and tried to scramble out of the way of the massive rock hurtling toward it, but it was too slow and was crushed under the weight of the boulder, driven deep under the earth where the tree roots snaked all over and around it, grab-bing and holding the Leshy in a perpetual chokehold.

The Leshy was not dead but trapped for eternity.

Or Worse.

The three friends stood there in disbelief of what they just witnessed. Robert did his best to explain to his friends everything he had seen and experienced: the Leshy, the trees attacking the Leshy, and also helping him escape. He explained that the BE-WARE THE LE sign actually meant BEWARE THE LESHY and that they should've paid more attention and been more careful when riding off-piste. Scott and Whitfield were amazed. They saw the monster hit the ground and get crushed by the rock. After see-ing that, they could see that believing that trees were sentient be-ings with thoughts and feelings wasn't very far-fetched. The three friends turned and faced the forest and thanked the trees for their help and for risking their own lives to help someone else. "You trees rule, and I am proud to have met you," said Robert solemnly, and all three friends bowed their heads in respect for the forest.

"Last one to the lodge buys dinner," cried Whitfield as the three friends started to ride down the rest of the mountain back to the ski lodge where they'd sit in front of a roaring fire and talk about the craziest day any of them had ever had.

And in the forest the trees whispered happily.

THE MOST BORING TOUR STORY

by Scott Ian, February 21, 2017

OBERHAUSEN, GERMANY—Anthrax rhythm guitarist Scott Ian got a most unwelcome surprise today when the underwear he put into the band's laundry bag after the previous night's show in Antwerp, Belgium, did not come back from the wash-and-fold they used in Oberhausen, Germany, that afternoon. Mr. Ian, upon finding that his stage underwear was missing, immediately questioned William Jarvis, the band's tour manager assistant and the person in charge of getting the laundry done: "Where is my underwear, Will?" Mr. Jarvis replied, "Are you sure you put them in the bag? Maybe you wore them back to the hotel after the show last night?" Mr. Ian, taken aback by such a nefarious claim, that he would wear his wet stage-worn underwear after the show, replied, "No, I didn't wear my gross, wet, gig-butt underwear back to the hotel. I threw them in the laundry bag." Mr. Jarvis promised he'd "get on it."

Frustrated by this dramatic turn of events on an otherwise seemingly normal day on tour, Mr. Ian reflected on the previous night's postshow activities and clearly remembered putting his underwear into the laundry bag. He was sure of it because the only underwear he wears on stage is manufactured by the brand Tommy John, and those were not in his travel bag. Mr. Ian questioned whether that evening's show could go on without his Tommy John underwear. What kind of effect would different underwear have on my ability to play this show? he wondered. "Could I possibly perform without the correct undergarments? Must the show go on?" he asked his bandmates.

His question was answered with a nervous silence and heads nodding in empathy for Mr. Ian's plight. Others had faced the horror of a missing sock or a shrunken T-shirt, but no one had ever been shaken to their foundation by a pair of missing underwear.

Mr. Ian, visibly upset by this disastrous turn of events, called for Mr. Jarvis, whispering, "Will, if they don't find my underwear, I will need to wear my backup pair. Will you please retrieve them for me?" And then Mr. Ian cried, "The show must go on!"

Thirty minutes later, having completed his preshow warmup, Mr. Ian, standing side stage, wearing unfamiliar underpants that were caught between his buttocks, was about to step on stage in front of a ravenous German heavy metal audience when Mr. Jarvis suddenly notified him that he had located his Tommy John underwear and that they would be "waiting for him after the show in the dressing room." The wash-and-fold had found them, and Mr. Jarvis had already deployed a runner to pick them up. Mr. Ian breathed a sigh of relief. He'd be able to soldier through that evening's show with a wedgie, knowing that his Tommy John underwear was safe and on its way home.

When reached for comment, Mr. Ian said, "I would like to thank God for giving man the ability to create such comfortable undergarments, and I would also like to express my gratitude to Mr. Jarvis and all those who helped him through this dreadful experience. I don't know what I would've done going forward without the extraordinary efforts made by Mr. Jarvis and others to retrieve this critical piece of equipment. Thank you all very much."

TSUNAMI

"There's a tsunami coming."

I wasn't sure I heard what Lani (Hammett, wife of Kirk) said correctly, so I asked, "What did you just say?"

Lani repeated, "There's a tsunami on the way from Japan. I just got a text from my father—he's watching the news. There was an earthquake off Japan, and a tsunami is coming our way." My wife, Pearl, and I were at dinner in Waikiki with Kirk and Lani when she got the text. We were just about done with dinner, it was 11:30 p.m., and traffic was already insane with people trying to get out of Waikiki when it suddenly hit home that this could be serious.

Pearl and I were on our babymoon in Hawaii. A babymoon is our last trip with just the two of us for a long time. It was a great vacation, super relaxing, doing nothing but laying on the beach, lounging in bed, eating room service, hanging with friends, and now running from a tsunami. A fucking tsunami? I'm from Queens. All I know about tsunamis is the giant wave in *Poseidon Adventure* and the footage from the Indian Ocean tsunami from 2004. I've seen what a tsunami is capable of.

We hadn't yet seen the Japanese footage from the tsunami created by the 9.0 Sendai earthquake, so at least we didn't have that to scare the shit out of us. Kirk suggested we follow them to his father-in-law's house inland, where we would be safe, but we decided to head back to our hotel on the North Shore because it was a safety zone for that area of the island. The tsunami was not expected until 3 a.m., so we figured we'd make it back in time; it was only a forty-five-minute drive once we got out of Waikiki. The only issue was that if they closed the road to our hotel that runs along the ocean for ten miles or so, we'd be fucked. *Fucked* meaning sleeping in our car somewhere inland on high ground but not drowned by a tsunami. We gambled.

We made it back to the hotel at 12:30 a.m. There were people everywhere; the lobby was packed. There were police and firemen giving directions to all the people who had evacuated from their houses on the North Shore. Hotel employees were taking groups of evacuees up into the hallways of the higher floors and were handing out blankets and pillows for them to camp out on.

Pearl and I got to our room and turned on CNN and saw the devastation in Japan. Unbelievable. Those images are still burned into my brain. After seeing the destruction caused by the sheer brutality of the tsunami in Japan we did start to worry. Would it really be safe here? The hotel is built up high on a rocky point and we're on the fourth floor. Was it high enough? Could the wave wipe out the lower floors of the hotel, causing the building to collapse? I called the front desk half a dozen times asking these questions. I told them I had a pregnant wife with me, and they reassured me each time that we'd be okay. Shit, I just saw Japan get demolished like Godzilla came through town. I was scared.

The local TV news was tracking the wave as it made its way across the Pacific. When it passed the Midway Islands the reports were varying from a four-foot to a twelve-foot wave. I learned that they have buoys out in the ocean that they get readings from. There's a big difference between a four-foot wave and a twelve-foot wave. Maybe someone needs to go check these buoys.

We just kept watching the ocean from our room, and we had a great view. At around 2 a.m. the hotel security announced over the PA that we had to close our balcony doors and shutters, leave our rooms, and move into the hallway. Pearl and I talked this over and decided to stay in our room. If something was coming at us, we wanted to see it. We figured we could make it into the hallway once we saw the wave. We were both amazingly calm considering that for all we knew a giant wave was barreling toward us at five hundred miles per hour.

I opened the door and saw that the hallway was packed with people from the lower floors. People had moved chairs and pillows from their rooms up with them to sit on. It was some scene—parents trying to get their kids to sleep in a hall packed with people and at the same time not freak the fuck out. I closed the door and tried to stay cool.

Pearl and I watched and waited. At 3:15 a.m. reports came in that Kauai got hit but no significant damage, as the wave was only three feet, though it could get bigger. We had about ten minutes until it hit. At this point I was really questioning whether we should've just gotten in the car and drove up the hill down the road from the hotel. How could I put my pregnant wife in danger like this? I was sweating.

Then we watched the ocean completely suck out about five hundred feet like someone rolling up a carpet.

It was nuts. All the water was gone, the ocean bottom and reef completely exposed, fish flopping around in the sand. We stood on the balcony waiting to see a huge wave come ripping toward the shore line.

And then it came.

A small wave maybe a foot high came speeding in, and then another and another on top of each other, moving really fast, flowing back into the empty space. This went on for a while, tiny wave after tiny wave. Pearl and I were nonplussed. Where was the tsunami? When it seemed like it had died down the reports on the news said that this was just the first wave and that the next wave could be twelve feet. I was starting to see a pattern here. I guess they have to scare the shit out of you in case it is bad so you take it seriously. Meanwhile at this point we're on the balcony shooting video of the ocean sucking out again and the small waves ripping back in. That's what happened over and over again for the next two hours. I looked out into the hallway to find it empty, and from our balcony we could see people leaving the hotel to go home.

At 5:45 a.m. we finally went to bed even though they were still saying "the big one" could come. We were very happy it didn't.

We woke up the next day and found out there was some damage on the Big Island and some damage to boats in some of the harbors across Hawaii as a whole, but all in all a nonevent, especially when compared to Japan.

Pearl and I got back to babymooning.

MADONNA

"Scott, Scott!"

Some woman was yelling my name from down the block on 53rd Street in New York City. I was standing outside the back door of the Roseland Ballroom with a bunch of friends after a Rancid show in October 1994. I kind of recognized the voice and could see by the stunned looks on some of my friend's faces (they could see over my shoulder) that it was someone serious. I generally don't turn around when someone is randomly calling my name from down the block, so I kept talking to my friends, and then again I hear her calling, "Scott, come over here!" By now my friend's eyes were bugging out of their heads. My curiosity piqued, I turned around to see Madonna standing next to a limo, waving me over. I calmly turned back around to my friends, playing it cool, acting like it was no big deal. Oh, it's just Madonna calling me over by my name to her limo, it happens every day, no big whoop. My poker face was holding on like the Alien face-hugger because on the inside I was having a full-on, pulse-pounding fuckaroo of a freak-out! *Holycrapit'sMadonnaholycrapit'sMadonnaholycrapit's Madonnaholycrapit'sMadonna and she is calling.* ME. OVER. TO. HER. CAR. WHAT THE FUCK IS GOING ON?

My friends were looking at me like I was nuts, and one of them said, "Dude, what are you waiting for? Get over there!"

I told them I'd be right back and tried to walk over as casually as possible, like I wasn't walking over to Madonna, standing next to her limo, waving at me, and calling my name. I could feel my friend's eyes on me as I approached her, my brain trying to deal with the mind-fuck of *how do I greet her?*

We had actually hung out once before, but this was Madonna. What do I do? Can't just shake hands. Do I presume there will be a hug? Will we be some high-fiving motherfuckers? Maybe a Euro-style double-cheek kiss?

Nope.

She grabbed me and pulled me into her arms and gave me a big fat smacker RIGHT ON THE MOUTH. Then she took my hand and pulled me into the back of the limo.

My mind was reeling . . .

She just kissed me and she's holding my hand and pulling me behind her into the car holycrapholycrapholycrap did my friends see all of this? (YES!) What is happening? Are we about to . . .

The End.

Hahaha, imagine?

Let's all just slow down, take a breath, and flashback to . . .

Two years earlier, somewhere in midtown Manhattan, I was sitting in the living room of the apartment that John Bush and I were sharing during the writing of the *Sound of White Noise* album. It was around 5 p.m., and I was just starting to recover from the previous evening's shenanigans when the phone rang.

"Hey, it's Guy O. What are you doing tonight?" Guy O is Guy Oseary, manager of Madonna, U2, Amy Schumer, and a bunch of other household-name artists. At the time Madonna had hand-picked Guy to run her new record label Maverick. This is before he signed Alanis Morissette and Deftones. We'd been friends for a few years, and he knew what a huge Madonna fan I was. Is that enough exposition?

"Hey Guy, what *am I* doing tonight?" I replied.

"I'll pick you up at your apartment at 6 p.m., then we'll head over to her house and pick her up and then go out to dinner, cool?"

"Umm, her? Who's her?" I asked ever so hopefully.

"Madonna. She wants to meet you."

Trying to contain my sheer excitement I somehow quickly answered, "Cool. See you at six."

I was not cool. I was far from cool. I was a stinking hungover mess. I had figured I had hours to get ready because, like a Spaniard, I hadn't planned on going out until at least midnight. Now I had less than an hour to get my shit together to go and meet Madonna. MADONNA. I had been a fan since "Burnin' Up" in 1983. I loved a good pop song, and it didn't hurt that the lady singing it was hot. I was hooked. I got to see her at Wembley Stadium on the Who's That Girl tour in 1987. I still have the T-shirt.

I got my ass in gear and jumped in the shower. As I was rushing through the three S's I realized I had a date that night with this model I was "seeing." Yeah, I was *that guy* back then, band dude dating a model. Sometimes you're too blind to see the cliché. And by blind I mean "in my twenties."

I called her, thinking it'd be no problem to cancel our date, that I'd just see her the next night and she'd be stoked for me because I was meeting Madonna.

"You're fucking joking vis me," she hissed at me in her Dracula-esque somewhere-from-Eastern-Europe accent after I told her what I was doing. "You're blowing me off for ... *Madonna*?" I tried to explain that it wasn't a date, it was Guy and I going out with her and what a big fan I was, and all I got from her was an extremely sarcastic, "Vell, have fun, see you." Click.

Normally I would've folded in a situation like this and called her back apologizing, not wanting to blow a good thing. But this was Madonna. I would've blown off Stephen King for this. Well, maybe not Stephen King, but it would be a tough decision.

Shitty phone call behind me, I got back to the business of getting ready. I was so nervous about meeting her that I was, for once in my life, actually worried about what I was going to wear. All I had on hand was my uniform: Levi's, a black T-shirt, and a leather jacket, so that would have to do.

Guy got to my apartment right on time, and we caught a cab up to Madonna's apartment on the upper west side. My nerves calmed a bit as we made small talk in the taxi. Guy was telling me our plan for the evening: dinner at some fancy-pants restaurant called Café Luxembourg, and then we'd head downtown to the Limelight to see Rage Against the Machine. Rage were still free agents and every label wanted them, and Guy was trying hard to get them for Madonna's label Maverick. Maybe bringing out the big gun, Madonna, and the smaller gun, the guy from Anthrax, would help his cause. Shit, I was just happy to be there.

We were stuck in traffic heading uptown. Someone had left a newspaper in the taxi, and flipping through it Guy saw an ad for the strip club Flashdancers and how they had some stripper *dancing* there with size 42GGG boobs. We talked about maybe checking that out for a goof at some point that evening as we finally pulled up to Madonna's building and headed up to her apartment.

As Guy knocked on her door all my nerves cooled off. Yes, I was really excited to meet Madonna, but the reality of my situation and surroundings put me into an almost Zen-like state of relaxation. She's just a person, I thought, a woman living in an apartment in the city just like millions of other people, and we're going to go out to dinner and chill just like millions of other people and then go see some live music just like . . . you get the idea. This wasn't going to be Madonna from the "Vogue" video opening the door; it was just going to be Guy's friend and employer Madonna. And then the door opened and

TITS.

Madonna's perfect tits.

Right there two feet away from me, shining like two brilliant suns through the sheer black top she was wearing. My eyes were caught in her tittie tractor beam, unable to look away. Madonna's boobs smiling at me as if to say, *She's just a person? She's just some schmuck like millions of others in this city? What are you, an idiot? She's fucking Madonna, you dummy. And look at us: Aren't we awesome? Go ahead and try to act like you don't notice Madonna's tits right in front of your face, hahahahahaha!* Her tits laughed at me like a supervillain who has just explained his whole plan to the superhero who he has trapped near the end of the movie and then, much like that old superhero movie trope, I broke free from the booby trap (hell yeah, I wrote that—I get a pass on that one!) and immediately refocused my eyes away from her tits and directly onto her eyes, which were smiling at me knowingly, I might add.

"Hi Scott, how do you like my tits?" is what my brain heard Madonna say, so I shook my head real hard like the Coyote in the old *Roadrunner* cartoons to clear it. What she actually said was, "Hi Scott, so nice to meet you. Guy has told me so much about you. Please come in," as she shook my hand and led us into her apartment.

Look at her eyes look at her eyes look at her eyes look at her eyes, I chanted over and over in my head. It would become my mantra for the evening, her tits always in my peripheral vision, taunting me.

Madonna offered us a drink and told us to make ourselves at home and then excused herself to finish getting ready to go out. "I'll give you the tour of the place before we go," she yelled from somewhere down the hall of her apartment. Apartment is really a deceiving noun for the space she lived in. Her "apartment" was five thousand square feet, much bigger than most houses.

A few minutes later Madonna came back into the living room, and much to my relief (and chagrin) she had put on a jacket over her sheer top. I could stop my mantra for the time being, her tits no longer shouting, "PAY ATTENTION TO US!" She showed me around her place, explaining to me how she had just purchased the apartment above hers and that she was going to break through the ceiling and put stairs in to create one ten-thousand-square-foot space. Ten thousand square feet on Central Park West. It'd be like living in Macy's, or Bergdorf Goodman as it's Madonna: Her place was incredible, immaculately designed and furnished—all that crap. I was especially fond of the original Dali she had hanging up.

Okay, I can hear you thinking, *Less* Architectural Digest, *more* Penthouse Forum. *Get back to her tits.*

Okay, okay, so we leave Madonna's apartment and get into the elevator, and Madonna looks at me and says, "Scott, Guy has been through this before, so he knows the procedure." I just nodded as she continued, "We're going to take the elevator to the basement garage where my car and driver and security are. When we pull out onto the street you'll notice three or four cars will pull out from in front of the building and follow us. They're paparazzi. They wait in front of my building twenty-four-seven. They're going to follow us to the restaurant, so as soon as we pull up in front of the restaurant you need to get out of the car quickly and go straight into the restaurant. Don't look at them, and don't engage them—that's what they want and that's what I have security for, got it?"

"Yeah, cool, okay, no worries. I got it."

I didn't have it.

All I could think of was that I was going to somehow trip Madonna as we got out of the car, and she'd be lying on the ground surrounded by photographers happily snapping away and thanking the bald jackass for the photo-op.

I sat there quietly sweating for the next few minutes trying to focus. I was going to be a ninja getting out of that car. Stealthy, moving like a cat from point A to point B, no mistakes. And then we were pulling up in front of the restaurant and the limo door was opening and I could see other cars pulling up behind us, in front of us, on the side of us, walling us in, and guys were running toward the entrance of the restaurant, cameras flashing like they were shooting King Kong, and I was out of the car, moving with my head down, security in front of me, shoving through the gauntlet of paparazzi, Madonna behind me, holding onto my jacket, Guy behind her, and we were getting bumped and pushed from the left and the right like a mosh pit had broken out in front of Café Luxembourg, except this wasn't fun. This was a crowd of dudes being physically aggressive at me and my friends, and I couldn't help myself as my instincts kicked in and I started yelling at the paparazzi, pushing back, grabbing their cameras—I was ready to fight them all. And then security pulled/pushed us through the doors and into the restaurant. Madonna was smiling at me. She could see how angry I had gotten and told me I had done well by not breaking someone's camera. I was still fuming. All I wanted to do was go back outside and beat paparazzi heads with their own cameras. I totally understood how Sean Penn must've felt. I had never had that kind of invasion of personal space before, and I didn't know how to deal with it. I still don't.

A few years ago a paparazzi was taking my picture as I was crossing a street in Beverly Hills, and I politely asked him to please not take my picture as I was holding my then two-year-old son. He followed me across the street, right next to me, camera in my face, and kept shooting, ignoring the fact that I was holding a child. If I didn't have my son with me, I wouldn't have cared about getting my picture taken, but my son has an expectation of privacy: he's not a public figure, *he's a child,* and I asked you nicely, jerk.

When we got to the other side of the street I told him he had no respect, that he was human garbage, and that if he didn't stop following us and taking pictures of my son, I was going to shove his camera up his ass. He looked at me like he didn't know what I was talking about and said, "Hey man, I'm just taking some pictures. Give me a break."

My left hand shot out and grabbed his neck while my right hand pistoned into his face over and over as his camera fell into the street and was crushed by a car, my son cheering, "Daddy smash!"

End awesome dream sequence.

"Fuck off," I growled at him, very Clint Eastwood–like through gritted teeth, hoping my son wouldn't hear me. He did. My son looked at me and said, "Uh-oh, Daddy." That made me laugh, and I kissed my boy and told him everything was okay. I was done, but the paparazzo wasn't. This guy continued clicking away until this elderly woman standing on the corner near us yelled at the guy, "You are a terrible person! Leave them alone." Finally the guy lowered his camera and said, "I didn't think it was such a big deal," and skulked off. I thanked the nice lady, and my boy and I walked off into the sunset.

Back at Café Luxembourg, we sat down to dinner, Madonna sitting across from me. She had taken off her jacket. I don't know how or why, but her boobs looked even better than they had before. Maybe it was the lighting in the restaurant or maybe it was just the fact that I WAS HAVING DINNER WITH MADONNA AND SHE WAS WEARING A SEE-THROUGH SHIRT.

I know, I know, I was thinking like an ass, but cut me some slack: it's Madonna.

I started up my mantra again, *look at her eyes look at her eyes,* and was relieved when the waiter brought menus over, giving me something else to focus on. Dinner ordered and a cocktail in hand, I was finally able to relax. It helped that Madonna was asking me question after question about my band and metal in general. She was picking my brain and engaging me in a way that was disarming and allowed me to feel like myself again—I could talk about my band all day long. The conversation continued all through the meal, and at some point I realized I wasn't freaking out anymore about her tits or about meeting her and finally stopped acting like a kid who just found his first *Playboy* magazine. She made me feel comfortable, like I was the only person in the room, and I could see that she really was a normal, down-to-earth, cool lady who also happened to be Madonna.

Dinner was winding down, and we got to talking about the plan for the evening. Madonna reminded me that the paparazzi were still outside and that we would do the same thing leaving the restaurant, straight into the car, no engaging them. I didn't get nervous about it; this time I really had it. At some point during dinner Guy and I were talking about the stripper with 42GGGs, and Madonna overheard us and said, "I want to go see her!" So the plan was set: we'd hit Flashdancers and then head downtown to the Limelight to see Rage Against the Machine.

Her security called the strip club to let them know we were coming and to be ready for the paparazzi. Getting Madonna in and out of places was like a military operation. We left the restaurant and had a much easier time getting into the car because her security and people who worked at the restaurant parted the paparazzi like the Red Sea, and we floated through unscathed.

It was a short drive to Flashdancers, and we beat most of the paparazzi there. We were walking into the club as most of them were getting out of their cars and running toward us, only to be blocked by the Flashdancers' giant security guys. Now that I was starting to get used to this whole paparazzi thing, I just smiled at them with my mouth while my eyes said, *Step-off, Gigantor—New Jack City* being all the rage back then.

If going to strip clubs is your thing and hooking up with a stripper is your goal, don't go to a strip club with Madonna. From the moment we sat down near the stage there was a line of strippers waiting to meet her. They'd step up, hug her, sit on her lap, and take a picture like they were meeting Santa Claus. If Guy and I had been hoping to hook up, we'd have been shit out of luck. They only had eyes for Madonna.

We hung out until the lady with the 42GGGs took the stage, and we watched her show. "Not for nothin', but those things look painful," I said, using some of my best colloquial New York–ese. Regardless, we were having fun, and so was the lady with the 42GGGs.

Mission accomplished, we said our good-byes and exited the club with a phalanx of beefy bouncers surrounding us on all sides. By this time I felt like I was developing a rapport with some of the paparazzi. They would yell questions like, "How was the club?" and I would flip them off.

Back in the car we sped down 7th Avenue to the Rage Against the Machine show. We were heading toward the Limelight, a rock club housed in what was formerly the Episcopal Church of the Holy Communion built in 1845. At some point in the 1970s the church was deconsecrated and turned into a drug rehab facility. When that business didn't work out the building was sold to a promoter and turned into a disco/rock club. God, drugs, and rock 'n' roll—it was always a house of worship. New York City rock clubs were still very debaucherous in the early nineties, and the building's gothic architecture and overall *churchiness* only added fuel to the fire. People really seemed to like getting fucked up in a church, so it was a great place to see shows.

We pulled up minutes before the band was going to start, I gave a quick flip of the bird to the paparazzi, and we were ushered into a private area above stage right, giving us a perfect view of the band and the audience. The house lights were still on, and I could see people I knew and people I didn't know looking up at us with confusion on their faces: *What was Scott doing with Madonna?* I'd let them think whatever they wanted. Who am I to burst *my* bubble? If memory serves, there may have even been an "Anthrax, Anthrax" chant from the audience, which in the moment was pretty flipping sweet—standing next to Madonna with the crowd worshipping me. Oh, the irony.

At this point in this tiny, dark unused crawlspace somewhere in my brain, the smallest kernel of an idea started to form: What if I could hook up with Madonna? What if I could go back to her apartment after the show? We'd had a good time all night—why not continue? As I was trying to figure out how to make that happen, the lights went out and the band hit the stage and I forgot what I was thinking about as RATM broke my brain as they crushed through their set of super-heavy rap/rock. The crowd went ape-shit. They'd never seen or heard anything so powerful, and it was easy to see that this band would be moving on to bigger and better things very soon.

The show ended, the lights came on, and before I even had a chance to recover from the spectacle I had just witnessed, Madonna was hugging me and Guy good-bye and goodnight, and she was gone.

Poof.

She disappeared into the dark recesses of the Limelight like a ninja.

My fan-boy crush would have to remain just that, as if I ever could've pulled off some magic move to cross that line. It was so ridiculous that I was laughing out loud. I couldn't be bummed about it. Guy asked me, "What's so funny?" and I told him I was telling jokes to myself.

Guy and I said goodnight, and I thanked him for including me in an amazing evening and that I owed him one big-time. I hopped in a cab, and when the cabbie asked me, "Where to, buddy?" I gave him my address. Normally I would've ventured out into New York City's seductive embrace, but I'd had enough. There was no way I could top that night out. I was drunk on the whole experience, and as they say, it's better to go out on a high note.

I woke up late the next morning and zombie-shambled into the kitchen for coffee. I poured a cup and sat down at the kitchen table. John had left that morning's copy of the *New York Post* open to Page Six (the celebrity gossip page) for me to see. There was a picture taken from the night before from the Limelight—someone had taken it from below, looking up at where we were standing. The picture was of Guy, Madonna, and my elbow. The photo had been cropped, cutting me out of the picture. There was a caption under the photo saying something about Madonna and Guy seeing Rage Against the Machine. There was nothing about the mysterious elbow on Madonna's right.

I laughed over my coffee and couldn't wait to tell the rest of the band about my crazy night out.

That was then. This is now.

Madonna has just kissed me on the lips and is holding my hand and I'm getting into her limo and my friends are all witnessing this and I'm wondering what in the world is about to happen and then I hear a heavily New York–accented male voice say, "Hi Scott. Nice to see you." Ron Delsener, the legendary New York concert promoter, is sitting in the back of the limo. Madonna says, "Scott, say hi to Ron!"

"Hi Ron. How are ya?" I mumbled, shaking the man's hand as the *Scott and Madonna, sitting in a tree, K-I-S-S-I-N-G* (yep, I was a child) fantasy world I had created crumbled into dust.

I got over it quickly, and it wasn't awkward to be sitting there because Anthrax had worked with Ron many times over the years, so conversation came easily. We talked about the Rancid show we had just seen and the resurgence of punk rock, with Ron holding court, telling tales about classic shows he'd done and a bunch of other stuff I can't remember, as all I could think about were my friends down the block. They didn't know Ron was in the car. Perception is everything.

I hung out with Madonna and Ron for about twenty minutes. They asked if I wanted to join them for dinner, but I politely declined, as I already had plans with my friends waiting for me outside. We said goodnight, and I got out of the car, stopping to nonchalantly adjust my clothes a bit before walking back to my friends. They were falling all over each other with curiosity as I rejoined their circle of inquiry, desperate to know what had transpired in the limo.

I just half smiled and said, "Nothing."

WE GAVE THE SUN
THE FINGER

I've always hated that stupid "What happens in Vegas stays in Vegas" slogan. I've spent a lot of time in Vegas over the years—on tour with Anthrax, playing poker tournaments, and Jerry Cantrell and I had a bar called Dead Man's Hand there for a year. This slogan was ubiquitous; I would hear it all day long. People actually say it out loud. I guess the ad company earned their money, but I have to ask: What's the point of having fun and not sharing? Sure, if your trip turns up a dead hooker in your hotel room and sparks a CSI investigation, keep your trap shut.

I was just in Las Vegas for my semiregular DJ gig at the Hard Rock Hotel. Yes, DJ Scott Ian. I've added another job on my résumé. If you're picturing some guy waving his hands in the air after pushing "play" on his MacBook Pro, playing EDM surrounded by his douche crew, that's not me. Well, the pushing "play" part is me. I'm not spinning records, but at least I'm choosing each song depending on the vibe of the people, and I only have around four minutes while a song is playing to make the decision on what comes next. I do take it very seriously. Like Eric B & Rakim said, "Move the crowd." After the gig I was walking through the Hard Rock lobby and heard some fanny-packer loudly slurring— unironically, mind you—"WhathappensinVegasstaysinVegas" as he had his picture taken in front of a display of Christina Aguilera's clothes. Yeah, better keep that quiet, you maniac, and erase that picture so the wife doesn't see it by accident. Sorry if that comes off a bit snarky. I'm no Hunter S. Thompson, but come on, people, you can do better than that.

Crazy fanny-pack got me thinking about a weekend not too long ago that involved a bit more than taking a picture in front of a bedazzled bra. It was one of those accidental weekends and started with a plan and a reason for me to be there . . .

I flew to Vegas to play in a charity poker tournament. I got to the Hard Rock Hotel the night before the tournament and planned on getting some dinner and then staying in so I'd be fresh for the event the next day. I texted my buddy Joe Bastianich (*Master Chef* judge and co-owner with Mario Batali of Eataly and a restaurant empire) to see if I could get a seat at one of his spots. He wrote me right back, telling me he was in town at his restaurant Carnevino at the Palazzo Hotel and inviting me over for dinner. For a second I thought about staying in and ordering room service. I should've thought longer on it.

I got in a taxi and headed over to the Palazzo. Joe met me in the bar of Carnevino and explained that he'd already eaten and was just about to have a meeting so I should eat dinner at the bar and then we'd hang out after and that I should have the La Fiorentina (sliced porterhouse): "It's the best in town."

I gorged myself on that delicious steak and then texted Joe to let him know I'd finished eating. He came out front and we headed back to a private room where Mario Batali was holding court. Mario. Alarm bells started ringing in my brain, and I had a moment of clarity, thinking I should politely phantom back to my hotel. I'd been out with Mario before, and the man was a force of nature. You had to commit to a night out with him, realizing no good would come of it—in the best of ways. The alarm bells were quickly quashed by a bear hug from the man: "How was the steak?" Mario smile-yelled at me over the Black Crowes he was cranking throughout the restaurant. "Have an Amaro—it's good for ya!" and a giant glass of Fernet Branca was shoved into my hand. I couldn't argue. One Fernet would be good for the meat sweats I was having from dinner.

One being the key word here.

I sat down and sipped my drink, realizing I was at a table with people who had already been drinking for hours. And not casual dinner drinking—this was Mario style. I'd sip my drink, and a waiter would appear and top me off. Another waiter came over with a Hagrid-sized wine glass three quarters filled with whatever red they were drinking. As soon as I'd make a dent in my wine it would get refilled. Fernet with a wine chaser. The night just got so much more interesting.

Tom Colicchio was there as well, so I was in full-on food-nerd mode sitting with him and Mario. Turns out Tom plays guitar and collects them as well. I remember that much of our conversation. What else did we talk about for an hour? No idea. What did I talk to anyone about for the next four hours? Ya got me. The Fernet and wine fountains never stopped flowing. I think at some point Mario had half the menu brought out, so like a Hobbit, I ate second dinner. My glasses emptied and magically refilled and I'd empty them again. The room was a swirl of voices and music and food and booze and too much of all of it, and we were doing our best to consume it all. There were no troughs at this Roman orgy, so I got up to find a bathroom and

Wet.

I'm wet. Why am I wet?

Where am I? Everything is white. It's so hot. I have no idea where I am. Why am I wet?

I blinked my eyes open, trying to adjust to the supernova brightness bleaching everything an uncomfortably hot white.

The sun was raging through the windows of my room at the Hard Rock. The Hard Rock. My room. How did I get here? The last thing I remembered was getting up from Mario's table to pee and then nothing. I was sweat-soaked in my clothes from the night before, the bed and blankets drenched underneath and on top of me. I had one sneaker on. As wet as I was, my mouth was dry as a kiln. There was a bottle of water on the nightstand, and reaching for it caused my rise up from the depths to speed up as the slightest movement made my head feel like Thor was pounding it with Mjolnir. Fully awake and in pain, I tried to take inventory.

It was 11:50 a.m. The charity event I was playing in started in ten minutes. I had no idea how I got back to the hotel. No memory at all of getting into my room. Blackout.

My wallet was on the nightstand. I checked it, and my cash and credit cards were all accounted for. There was a crumpled piece of paper next to the money. Taxi receipt. Somehow I had gotten in a taxi from the Palazzo at 5:08 a.m.

My laptop was open to the Ultimate Bet online poker site. I logged in and saw that I had played online at 6:18 a.m. for about forty-five minutes. I had won quite a bit of money as well. I checked my hand history, where you can see all the hands you played and how you played them to see how I had managed that, and apparently a drunk Gorilla Grodd had taken over my brain and the ultra-aggressive, abusive-style hold 'em he played was very successful. I made a mental note of that for future poker endeavors.

My timeline piecing together, I did a quick scan of the room: no blood or puke—check. No other humans alive or dead—check. Remains of a cheeseburger and fries all over my bed—check.

Still sweating, I slowly got out of bed. There was no time to shower or even change my clothes. I quickly brushed my teeth, found my other sneaker, and threw on a hoodie, hoping it would at least mask the fact that I was in the same clothing from the night before. Oh, and also maybe put a layer between the booze stench coming off me and the people I'd be sitting next to at the poker table.

I made it out of the room and down the hall to the elevator. That's when I realized I was still drunk. The initial clearheadedness and ability to take stock of my surroundings I had felt when I first woke up was now replaced with a loopy giddiness that wasn't all that terrible. My head still had a vice on it; I'd need to deal with that immediately. I got off the elevator and kept my head down, not because I didn't want to be recognized but because I had to watch my feet as I walked so I wouldn't trip over them. I didn't want to be late for this event, especially for a lame reason like being a hungover pile of crap.

I got to the venue and was relieved to see I wasn't late. They were still registering people to play. The tournament was for a charity that supported injured soldiers returning from Iraq and Afghanistan. MMA superstar Randy Couture was hosting it, and 150 people entered the tournament—celebs, poker pros, MMA fighters, and the public. It was a great turnout for a worthy cause.

I got my seat assignment and sat down at my table, oozing Fernet from my pores. I figured I wouldn't last long in the tournament, bust out, and go back to bed was my plan.

I start to focus on actually playing cards and look around the table at my opponents, and sitting right across from me is David Wells. As you know from another story in this book, I am a huge Yankee fan, and Boomer (his nickname) was my favorite player on those 1997–1998 teams. He played the game hard and partied even harder. Wells was a throwback and embodied everything I loved about seventies baseball.

I found it difficult to concentrate on the poker game. I was next-day drunk and sitting at a table with one of my heroes. I wanted to talk to him, but I never want to bother anyone. My nerves were shot. I made an adult decision to order a Bloody Mary to take the edge off. I was very quickly halfway through my beverage when Wells asks me what I'm drinking. An icebreaker! I told him it was a Bloody Mary, that I usually don't drink so early, but I needed some help, as I had just got up and barely made the tournament. Turns out he was in the same boat as me. He said he had ordered a real drink when he first sat down but didn't want to be "that guy" so he changed his order to a soft drink. When he saw me order booze he figured that made it okay. So now that we had established that we were both degenerates, we became fast friends. The waitress was instructed to keep 'em coming, and I was already feeling better and having a blast picking his brain about all things Yankee and baseball in general—his love of Babe Ruth, his hatred of Joe Torre, cranking metal in the locker room, and partying with the notorious New York Mets. Of course I asked him about the perfect game he pitched in 1998. He didn't seem to mind talking about anything; the man had no sacred cows. Wells pitched the fifteenth perfect game in baseball history. There had always been rumors that he was high when he took the mound that day. And after he pitched the perfect game he partied so hard the next four days that he didn't make it out of the first inning of his next start.

We're talking and talking, and the hours slip by, and somehow Wells and I both make the final table. I was short stacked in chips and finished tenth, busted by poker legend Phil Gordon. Wells busted in eighth place. They raised $100,000 for the charity.

Wells asked if I was *done* or did I want to meet up in a few hours for dinner? I could sense the hidden agenda behind the word *done,* meaning was I down to party like a big boy or was I going to puss out. I told him I needed to take a nap and shower and then I was up for anything. This was my chance to hang with a Yankee!

I woke up from my nap feeling almost human again. I met Wells for dinner, and he was a man with a plan. Dinner turned into drinks, drinks turned into the Spearmint Rhino strip club, Spearmint Rhino turned into the 40 Deuce burlesque club, 40 Deuce turned into us walking through the parking lot of the Hard Rock Hotel with triple vodkas for the road in hand on the way to a club called Body English, where I called my lady Pearl to let her know what was happening and that I'd be taking a later flight home in the afternoon, and then Wells grabbed the phone out of my hand to manically harangue her for ten minutes yelling about what a great time we were having and how crazy I was and to not worry because he was taking good care of me. Pearl was unfazed.

By this time I swear I could see actual fire in Wells's eyes. If I hadn't been with him all day, I would've been scared of the dude, and even then he was a little scary. I would never have wanted to face him in a game if he was pissed off.

We had a table at Body English with a bottle of vodka waiting for us, and Wells told me that Jason Giambi was on his way to meet us. Boom. I just doubled down on my Yankee night out. The three of us finished that bottle, and then that turned into us heading (sans Giambi) to another strip club, and all of this became me doing my best to keep up with this six-foot-five badass motherfucker for twenty hours.

We gave the sun the finger and then said our good-byes. I headed to my room, and this time I was conscious of the fact that I was going to sleep.

I made my flight home and called Wells that afternoon to thank him for the good time. I asked him if at any time during the evening he had thrown a fastball at my head. Can a hangover kill you? This one certainly tried to. No hair of the dog this time—I sweated it out for three days and didn't drink for a month.

Thanks for letting me share.

Yep, it really happened. Reveling in Yankee glory with Jason Giambi and David Wells. Courtesy Scott Ian.

THE WALKING DEAD

My Life as a Zombie

"Okay, so Andrew is going to be fighting the walkers, and they are going to back him up to right in front of where you are laying under the garbage. As soon as he is within your reach I want you to lunge out with your hand and grab his leg. And I mean really grab it, as hard as you can, and don't let go until he rips his leg out of your hand. Got it? Then you start crawling out, okay?"

I was trying hard to listen to director/executive producer/effects legend/metalhead/friend Greg Nicotero give me direction for my scene with Rick (Andrew Lincoln) and Carl (Chandler Riggs). I really was trying to pay attention—the last thing I wanted to do was screw up and have the whole production waiting on *Greg's friend* to get it right. My comprehension issue stemmed from it being very hard for me to get past the idea that I was actually IN *The Walking Dead.*

IN IT.

I was lying under a pile of garbage, made up as a walker, about to attack the main character of the show. This was truly the biggest who-the-hell-let-me-in-here-moment of my life.

Ever since I was a kid imitating Flyboy's zombie walk from George Romero's *Dawn of the Dead,* I've spent countless hours thinking about getting to be a zombie in a movie or TV show. Dream big, kids—it pays off! My path to zombie-dom was a long one. You don't just get made up by an effects guy and bam, you're a zombie. No, it takes a lot of hard work and disappointment, and ultimately it's your love for the genre that will allow you to triumph and represent the undead.

The Walking Dead premiered on Halloween 2010, and it quickly tapped into a heretofore-unknown vein, the mainstream's love of zombies. Who knew? I don't need to tell the story of how a horror genre-specific show based on a comic book became the biggest show on television. All of that is well documented and written about by actual television writers. This story is about how a zombie-obsessed nerd became one.

Not long after *The Walking Dead* took a big bite out of our TV watching habits I got a call from my agent, asking when I'd be in New York City because there was a show being put together, some kind of "talk show about zombies," and the producers wanted to see me. It just so happened I was in New York City, and I was intrigued—a talk show about zombies? I could do that all day. Shit, I already did that all day and no one was paying me for it. The next day I spoke to a producer who told me that the idea for the show was a *Walking Dead* postshow. They wanted a couple of guys sitting around talking about the episode they just watched. I thought he was kidding. "That's a show?" I asked him. I wasn't being a jerk about it; I was genuinely curious. He told me they had Chris Hardwick as the host, and my role would be zombie expert and field reporter. He also told me to not talk about this with anyone; it was top secret. I was trying to visualize the show in my brain, like a football postshow where the hosts discuss the game and give replays of the best plays. Like if Chris and I watched *Dawn of the Dead* and then broke it down afterward: "What a movie, Chris! Let's see that helicopter blade-cut through the zombie's head again in slow motion." "Oh yeah, Scott! That was awesome. And how about that biker who just had to have his blood pressure taken right in the middle of the mall surrounded by zombies? What the hell was he thinking? Let's take another look and see where he went wrong." Was there really an audience for that?

I couldn't believe we were having this conversation. An actual TV producer was telling me he wanted me to be a "zombie field reporter" on a pilot episode for a not-yet-titled *Walking Dead* postshow. That's a dream job I couldn't have conjured myself, even in my wildest fantasies. And I was already friends with Chris from way back in the nineties when I first saw him doing stand-up comedy in Los Angeles, so that made it even better. I told the producer I'd love to be on that show and when and where did they want me?

A couple of days later I was on the set of Andy Cohen's *Watch What Happens Live* show watching some stagehands redecorate Andy's set with some horror accoutrement, zombifying it. Chris and I talked to the producers, who ran us through what we'd be doing. It couldn't have been easier. We talked about the episode we had just watched and speculated on the characters' fates. Chris introduced my field segment, and I talked about that (even though it hadn't been shot yet), and we basically nerded out for thirty minutes. The producers said it went great, and we all went out for food and drinks. Easy peasy. Chris and I were all smiles as we talked about the idea of doing this show. It was really too good to be true.

My field reporter segment was going to be filmed the following week in Los Angeles, where Greg Nicotero was directing the first *Walking Dead* webisodes about the life of the "Bicycle Girl" zombie, the crawling torso zombie that Rick puts out of her misery in episode one, season one. The webisodes were going to be her backstory. My job was to report from the set, show how things are done, and get made up to be a walker. Yeah, I know, tough job.

I wasn't just excited about this gig; I was losing my mind. And I'd be working with effects master Greg Nicotero. Cofounder of the KNB EFX Group, the man is a fucking legend. It'd be easier to list the movies he hasn't worked on. I knew Greg from the late 1980s; we had met through our mutual friend and horror nerd Kirk Hammett. We had one night out in particular that bonded us as lifelong friends in the early 1990s.

Kirk was staying at the Chateau Marmont in bungalow 3. That's the bungalow where John Belushi died. Kirk, Greg, my friend Rich, and I got very drunk that night, and when we got back to the bungalow we decided we'd go on a hunt for Belushi's ghost. Yep, we were that drunk. First we had to get back into the bungalow, as Kirk had lost his key and we were all too drunk to find our way back to the front desk through the dark labyrinth-like grounds of the Chateau. Rich fixed that problem by punching his hand through a pane of glass in the door and reaching in and opening it from the inside. I still don't know how he didn't cut the shit out of himself. Maybe Belushi's spirit was watching over us and enjoying the mayhem. We started searching the bungalow for signs of I don't even know what, anything that seemed to evoke Belushi. This was at least ten years after he had died, and the place had obviously been cleaned thousands of times, but in our compromised states we weren't thinking clearly. Mostly we were all just giggling and stumbling around. Greg—at least I think it was Greg—found a door that led to a space underneath the bungalow. Jackpot! We found a flashlight (I have no idea where we found a flashlight), and all of us headed through the mystery door and down the steps into the basement. There was a dirt floor and some trash littered throughout the space. I found an old Budweiser can and that's all we needed—it was 100 percent absolutely Belushi's old beer can. We had proof! I was yelling, "It's proof, it's proof!"

Proof of what, I have no idea now, but in that musty dark basement it meant everything in the moment. I was holding it up over my head triumphantly as we all ran back up the stairs yelling that we found it. Short-attention-span drinkers that we were, we were onto something else pretty much right after we found the beer can. We'd make shitty ghost hunters.

Back to the zombie postshow, I got to the set of the webisodes and was immediately sent to the makeup trailer to start the process of transforming me into a walker. I met Garrett Immel from KNB, and he explained how they had already made some of the pieces they would put on my face just using photos of me as reference, which would speed up the process a little bit. He wasn't starting from scratch and had a good idea of what he wanted to do to my face, walker-wise. Usually they would use a life cast of the actor's head to make the pieces, but I had not had one of those done (yet).

Even with some of the pieces already made, it still took about three and a half hours to glue all the pieces on and paint them. I loved every minute of it. I didn't want Garrett to finish. I've read about actors who hate having to spend so much time getting made up for a role as well as actors who love it and totally go with it. And they're getting paid millions to do it. I would show up and do this for free just because it was that much fun. Seriously, if I could get made up by KNB every day, I would.

Looking in the mirror and seeing a different face looking back at me was awesome. It felt liberating. Any nerves I had about having to act disappeared into my new face. My only issue was that my eyes were still my eyes, distracting from the brilliant job Garrett had done. I told him my eyes made my new walker face just look like my old face. He told me not to worry: once I had the contact lenses in that would all change. But I was worried about the contact lenses. I'd never had lenses in before this, and like most people, I'm sensitive to stuff getting put into my eyes. I met with the lens expert, and she calmly talked me down off the ledge. If she could put lenses in Johnny Depp's eyes (she was his personal lens person), I guess I could trust her.

I sucked it up and did my best to relax. Unlike getting the makeup on my face, having the lenses put in was not enjoyable. It took multiple attempts on each eye, mainly because I was so nervous. I could barely deal with the eye drops she used to lubricate my eyeballs before the lenses were put in. Then she's telling me to look up and off to one side, and I'm sweating and trying to breathe through it, but there's a finger in my eye and the lens feels giant and weird, and then it's in and she tells me to close my eye and move it around. I could feel the lens—no pain, just the size of it. The lenses she made for me were almost opaque and are larger than the everyday contacts people wear. She told me to open my eye, and I could barely see. And that was just my left eye. I still had an eye to go. The second lens was a little easier, as I knew what it'd feel like. With both lenses in I really couldn't see. I had a production assistant who was supposed to help me walk around set, but that made me feel lame, so I walked very slowly and deliberately. The lenses were helping me get into walker mode. Method acting! And they looked great. The discomfort had been worth it. I didn't look like me to me anymore. Well, except for my beard. We talked about what to do about my beard while I was in the makeup chair. It's very recognizable and wouldn't take that keen of an eye to spot me. They didn't have a piece made to go over my chin, so I said, "Why can't the walker just be me? I was bitten protecting my family, and now there's a Scott Ian zombie walking around." We were probably really overthinking the whole thing, but hey, it's all about the details. And now I had a backstory!

I shambled from the makeup trailer over to "walker boot camp," where Greg introduced me to a walker named Joe Giles. Joe worked for KNB and was their number-one walker. He was one of the first people they tested to be a walker on the show and became their go-to guy for really intense, close-up walker action. Joe had that shit down. He asked me to show him my walk. I wasn't nervous about this part; I had been practicing and visualizing

It's all in the eyes. On the set of the "Bicycle Girl" webisodes. Courtesy Scott Ian.

this moment since I was eight years old! I did my walk, slow, jerky, letting extremities hang, leaning where weight would sag to one side, imagining my brain was disconnected from my body, that I had no control over my movements. I even loosened my left shoe so I could bend my foot inward at the ankle, creating the effect of my shoe meeting the ground sideways so it looked like I was walking on a broken ankle. I finished my walker runway walk and anxiously waited for Joe to weigh in. He smiled through his completely torn-off cheeks and said, "You got it. Excellent. I have no notes." Triumph! Validation from a zombie expert! I had passed walker boot camp with decaying colors.

I asked Joe what mistakes the walker extras make on set, and he told me the biggest zombie no-no is the Frankenstein's monster, arms up in front. That'll get you fired from the ranks of the undead immediately.

Having graduated walker school, I was ready for my walker debut. The set was on an actual street they had closed off in the West Adams area of Los Angeles. West Adams is an old neighborhood

With Joe the pro. Courtesy Scott Ian.

by Los Angeles standards. It was one of the first areas developed after people started moving out of the downtown area in the late 1800s, and by people, I mean rich white dudes who built beautiful craftsmen houses and awesomely creepy mansions, most of which are still standing. It had the right vibe for shooting horror.

I headed down the block to the house where they were shooting the scene and met with Greg. He explained the scene: "You'll be walking down the street toward the house. Hannah"—the woman that would become the Bicycle Girl zombie—"and her two kids are going to come running out and run right past you. You'll turn and follow them."

I could do that. We did three or four takes, and then Greg had me do a few more turns because he wanted to get a good close-up shot of my face. I could've shot the scene all day long. I would've done anything—bite someone, get torn in half, or rip someone's guts out and eat them. I was committed. Even the contact lenses weren't bothering me anymore as long as they put drops in my eyes every fifteen minutes.

Already an old pro, I asked if I could keep the makeup on and hang out and watch the rest of the shoot. A camera team was filming me for my field report, so they were fine with being able to get more content of me on set. I watched Joe shoot his scene; he surprises Hannah, biting her arm after she gets in a car she is hoping to use to get herself and children to safety. Hannah shoots Joe in the head and runs out of the car.

It was so cool. I hoped that someday I'd get to do a scene where I got shot in the head—or worse.

I got worse.

I hung around another hour watching them shoot. During one shot Greg yelled, "More blood! I need more blood!" I loved having a job where people yelled things like that. I talked at the camera about my experience for the field report and was done. Garrett asked if I wanted to come back to the trailer to take the makeup off, and I asked if I could wear it home. I had the idea to have the camera crew follow me home and film me walking into my house, hanging out with my wife, Pearl, and holding my then two-month-old son, Revel, just another day in the life of a walker.

Greg said if the makeup wasn't bugging me, it was fine with him if I wore the makeup home. They gave me the stuff they use to dissolve all the glue and a couple of tubes of the makeup remover and told me to take a really hot shower to take it all off in there. I got some very strange looks at red lights on my way home. The crew filmed me holding my son, asking him if he wanted to eat guts for dinner. He didn't even blink looking at me—no fear at all. That's my boy!

Father of the year! Courtesy Scott Ian.

And we got a great picture of the three of us in front of the fireplace that we used as our Christmas card that year. Father of the year, right here.

I was so excited to have been a part of *The Walking Dead* webisodes and could hardly wait for them to air in October before the season two premiere. I had already given up on the talk show thing,

We're a happy family! Courtesy Scott Ian.

figuring they cut together the pilot and it was a no-go. I didn't care: if getting made up and being in the webisodes was all I got to do, I was stoked with having been able to have that amazing experience.

Then my agent called.

The Talking Dead was a go.

"Wow! Holy crap, that's awesome! They liked what we did! Cool title as well!" I excitedly said to my agent. "I am fucking thrilled! My dream job is becoming a reality! I'm going to be on a TV show talking about zombies and get to be a part of that world on the inside!"

I was so excited that I wasn't paying attention to my agent as she was trying to get my attention: "Scott, hold on, hold on, listen. There's something I need to tell you . . ."

"Sorry, I'm just so excited about this. What is it?"

She got quiet for a few seconds and said, "*The Talking Dead* is a go, but not with you."

"Huh? What? I don't understand. What do you mean?" I nervously replied, my excitement running out of me faster than the Flash and a hot pit of anxiety growing in my belly.

"They're just going with Chris as the host, no field reporter/ zombie expert. They thought you were great—they're just going a different way with the show. I'm so sorry," she said, trying to let me down easy. I felt like I'd fallen off a cliff onto the sea-battered rocks below.

I mustered up a reply, "Umm, okay. No worries. Thanks for telling me," and I hung up.

Fuck.

I was bummed, but I was already climbing out of the rocks. I still got to be in the webisodes, and the reality of being able to be on a weekly show was not reality. My schedule with Anthrax would never allow for that. I wasn't thinking of that when I was fantasizing about getting paid to talk on television about zombies. And really, I wasn't missing out on anything because who would watch a *Walking Dead* talk postshow?

NEW YORK, NY, OCTOBER 16, 2016—Days before the highly antici- pated season seven premiere of *The Walking Dead* AMC announced that the series, the number-one show on television among adults eighteen to forty-nine for the last four years, had been renewed for an eighth season, premiering in late 2017 and kicking off with the one hundredth episode of the franchise. All sixteen episodes of *The Walking Dead* season eight will be followed by *Talking Dead,* the live after-show hosted by Chris Hardwick, which is the highest-rated talk show on television and number-two show on cable, behind *The Walking Dead.*

Who indeed.

Talking Dead became the highest-rated talk show on televi- sion. More people watch *Talking Dead* than almost all the late- night talk shows—Colbert, Kimmel, Fallon, Meyers, and so on— combined. Congratulations to my buddy Chris Hardwick, the king of talk shows! This shows you what I know about programming television. I'll stick to watching it.

Okay, back to October 2011, *Walking* and *Talking Dead* were starting their takeover of the airwaves, I was on tour for our *Worship Music* album, and life moved on. Seven months later, out of the blue, I got an email from Chris Hardwick.

☆ **Chris Hardwick**   April 11, 2012 at 6:25 AM   CH
To: SCOTT IAN   Details

Hey man! Top secret idea here, but we might be doing a make-up fx show with Fangoria. Essentially, you'd go to someone like Nicotero, for example, (or another make-up god) and he'd give you a basic walkthru of creating specific make-up fx. We may initially shoot 5 and see how they do. We'd obviously work around your schedule. If interested, we can be more official and have our biz people reach out to yours. Just wanted to gauge your interest first. I think you'd be great for this.

Hope you're well!
ch

--
nerdist.com I Nerdist Channel I Nerdist News I @nerdist

I don't know why Chris was up at 6:25 a.m. thinking about me, but I sure am happy he was. I immediately replied, telling Chris I was definitely interested, and soon after that my show *Blood & Guts* (changed to *Bloodworks* after Nerdist stopped working with Fangoria and started working with Legendary to produce the show) was born. Instead of getting to talk about zombies on television, I was going to get to be made up every episode and get killed or maimed in some awesome way by the top effects guys. Chris and the folks at Nerdist introduced me to Jack Bennett, who they got to direct/produce the show, and we hit it off right away. We were nerdmates. Jack brought in a DP named Justin Cruse, another nerdmate, and we were hip deep in gore in no time.

Over the course of the show I've had my head chainsawed in half by Jerry Constantine. I got to bash a zombie's head in with a pipe and run over a zombie's head with a car at the KNB shop with Greg Nicotero. I got turned into a Jewish Jerry Garcia who, in an homage to *Candid Camera*, takes a guitar off the wall at a guitar shop on Sunset Boulevard, plugs it into an amp, and plays Anthrax and Slayer way too loud to the amazement of the customers and the dismay of the store management before I walk out with the guitar and get chased down the street. Jennifer Aspinall made all that happen. I got a knife through the face by Robert Hall. I was shot, blown up, and taught how to use a flame-thrower by Ron Trost. Decapitated by a gorilla? Yep, that was with Tom Woodruff Jr. and Alec Gillis. I had my face ripped off by Larry Bones and my fingers bitten off by a troll with Mike Elizalde. Vincent Van Dyke turned me into the devil who then grants my younger self's wish to be "just like Angus" by impaling me on a Gibson SG guitar neck the same way Angus Young is on the cover of AC/DC's *If You Want Blood* album. I was turned into a Deep One from Lovecraft's *The Shadow over Innsmouth* and Jack the Ripper by the amazing Joel Harlow.

Had enough? Hell no.

I was disemboweled by that evil little fucker Chucky thanks to Tony Gardner. I got drunk in the afternoon with Dan Harmon (talking about his stop-motion animation company Starburns that made *Anomalisa*) and then got to see a stop-motion miniature of me murder the Easter Bunny. I spent two days with the legendary Rick Baker, who regaled me with amazing stories about his work (Eddie Murphy is one of those actors who loves to get made up) and showed me his incredible paintings. I went to the *Game of Thrones* set in Belfast and got turned into a fucking White Walker by their makeup wizard Barrie Gower. That's a lot of blood and guts and not even close to all of it. Thank you, gentlemen, for making dying so much fun.

Earlier in this tale I said that becoming a zombie "takes a lot of hard work and disappointment, and ultimately it's your love for the genre that will allow you to triumph and represent the un-dead." It had been almost three years since the disappointment of not getting on the *Talking Dead* turned into the delight of making *Bloodworks*, which came out of my love for the genre, and all of that led up to me asking Greg Nicotero and the Nerdist producers going through proper channels and asking the network AMC if we could bring our little *Bloodworks* show down to Atlanta to do an episode with *The Walking Dead.* Greg had already invited me down to get made up and be a walker, but I wanted more than that—to do an episode of *Bloodworks* with a show as big as *The Walking Dead,* well, that would really put us on the map, getting to be a part of the biggest show on television. That was what I wanted. And on August 1, 2014, they said yes. I was going to be a walker in an episode on the fifth season of *The Walking Dead.* Jack and I were thrilled; this was a really big deal on so many lev-els. They were giving us access no other media gets, but we were under strict guidelines: we were not allowed to shoot; AMC had a camera crew to shoot, and then they would supply us the foot-age. No problem. We were not allowed to post any pictures from set or even talk about what we did until after the episode aired. No problem. We couldn't air our episode until after the episode aired. No problem. There wouldn't be a problem—we would've done anything they asked us to make this happen. This was "The Show." Doing the webisodes was great, but this was the real deal. Like in baseball when a minor league player gets drafted up to the majors, he's made it to "The Show."

Greg needed my life cast sent to the KNB shop in Los Angeles so they could start working on my walker. I'd had my head cast twice for episodes of *Bloodworks* at this point. The first time I had it done they didn't put enough Vaseline or whatever they use to keep the alginate from sticking to my chest hair, and when they pulled it off it was like the scene in the *40-Year-Old Virgin* when Steve Carell gets his chest waxed. I cry a little just thinking about it.

This time around my walker was going to be sans beard. Scott Ian isn't walking around in Atlanta, so they would need to make a chin appliance to glue over it. Other than that detail I didn't want to know what they had planned for my walker; I wanted to see it all for the first time in the makeup chair on set. Everything was coming together; the only piece missing was when. It had to be an episode that Greg was directing—he was directing four episodes in season five—and it had to be on a date when I wasn't on tour. With both of our schedules so fluid it took a lot of juggling and planets aligning to finally nail down October 6 as the shoot date. I couldn't believe this was happening.

MONDAY, OCTOBER 6, 2014

THE WALKING DEAD EPISODE: 512 (airdate tbd 2015)

RUN OF SHOW:

5:15 a.m.—CALL TIME AT BASECAMP / AD TRAILER. Yes, bright and early, though it will still be dark out!

5:18 a.m.—WARDROBE. I will meet you at the AD trailer upon arrival to sign NDAs and escort you to Wardrobe.

5:48 a.m.—MAKEUP

7:18 a.m.—CAMERA READY

7:30 a.m.—REHEARSAL

8:00 a.m.—SHOOTING. You are in the first two scenes shooting this day.

1:00 p.m.—LUNCH. You may be wrapped by this time but are more than welcome to stay and join us for lunch.

EPK crew will arrive at 5 a.m. to be camera ready as
previously discussed for wardrobe/hair/makeup process
and b-roll of scenes. You will have access to basecamp
b-roll immediately through AMC PR. Access to scene
b-roll will be closer to airdate, as directed by AMC PR.

Getting that email of the schedule the week before the shoot
was so cool that it made it real in my brain. I was really doing this.

I flew to Atlanta the night before the shoot and took a taxi to
the hotel, where I met my manager, Mike, as well as Charlie from
the band, who came down with his daughter Mia. They are all
huge fans of the show as well, and the opportunity to come to the
set was too good to pass up. I tried to get to bed early, as I had a
5:15 a.m. call time, but I was too excited to sleep. I barely got two
hours and then was on my way to Senoia where *The Walking Dead*
sets are. It didn't matter that I hadn't slept; I had so much adrenaline running through me that I was fully amped.

I got to the set right on time. It was still dark and was cold, in
the low thirties. Security directed me over to where the dressing
room trailers were. The set was very quiet; no one was around to
ask what to do. Craft services (catering) were already set up, so
I grabbed the largest coffee I could find and waited for someone
to come and open up the dressing room trailer. I was with Mike,
Charlie, and Mia, all of us standing outside in the dark, freezing
and laughing about how glamorous big-time TV is. After about
ten minutes of that, someone from the production came by and
said, "You guys must be freezing! I'll open your dressing room—
there's heat in there." I wasn't bothered—I would've stood out in
the cold all day to get to be a walker. But we all crowded into my
little room to get warm, and I figured the whole day was going to
be a lot of hurry up and wait.

Wrong.

There was a knock on the dressing room door, and someone from the costume department brought my bespoke walker wear in for me to try on (I had sent my sizes weeks before). Looking filthy in my zombie best, I was whisked over to the makeup trailer to be transformed.

I met Kevin Wasner from KNB EFX, and we got right into it. I asked him what he had planned for me, and he pointed to a model of my head with the pieces they had made for my walker face. It was a full head application, or what they call "hero makeup" because there was going to be close-up shots of my face. The details were incredible, the open wounds on my head were beautiful, and the way they had my spine showing through on the back of my neck was so cool. Look at the pictures, as my words don't do justice to the artistry involved. The makeup took four hours, which for me flew by. I am fascinated with the process of transformation by makeup effects, as a fan and as a subject, and I find the experience to be deeply satisfying. It's like getting to wear the ultimate Halloween costume.

I emerged from the makeup trailer into the now-warm and sunny morning a new man, brutally handsome in an undead sort of way. I was taken straight over to the costume department, where they added the finishing touches to my clothes, airbrushing the dried blood in all the appropriate places, and giving my look an overall aged feel. The attention to detail is really incredible, with the different departments in synergy to create the best the genre has ever seen.

And then I was ready for contacts. As you know from my experience on the webisodes, I'm never thrilled about having contacts put in, but in this scenario I was a pro-lens guy. They popped those suckers right in, and there was no grief from me. I was ready for my close-up, Mr. Nicotero.

A real big-league Walker. I made it to the show! Courtesy Scott Ian.

It was a short drive over from base camp to where they were shooting. I headed right over to the set, where they were rehearsing the fight choreography of the scene with Andrew Lincoln and Chandler Riggs. I immediately noticed that Andrew had shaved the beard he had in the previous season. A detail like this would be big news in the *Walking Dead* fan world. Being the nerd I am about the show, I was stoked to have this inside info before anyone else, and of course I was speculating about why he shaved. Nerd! Another cool detail I noticed was every time they'd rehearse the fight, at the end of the scene Andrew and Chandler would help the actors playing the walkers get up off the ground and ask if they were okay. I noticed this all over the set that day. The walkers were very well taken care of. I thought that was really cool. Andrew later told me that they're always nice to the walkers, that they are all just working together to make a great show and the people playing the walkers work really hard in tough conditions under all that makeup.

Greg came over to me, gave me a hug, and looked me over, his keen eye taking in every detail of my makeup and costume. He thought I looked great, but they'd just do some touch-ups right before we shot so the makeup looked fresh on camera. Greg introduced me to Andrew and Chandler, and we shook hands and said hello—they were both very cool. Greg went right back to work laying out the scene again: Andrew and Chandler would be fighting the four walkers that came out of the woods, and they will kill three of them quickly and then Andrew, struggling with the last walker, gets backed up to where I was underneath the pile of garbage, and then I reach out and grab his boot. Andrew pulls away from me, and then I crawl my upper half out of the garbage, reaching for them, but I can't crawl all the way out because my legs are stuck. I keep reaching for them, and Andrew, just about to kill me, defers to Chandler when Chandler asks for the metal pole and Chandler puts the pole through my head. Greg asked if we were all good with the scene, and we were, so he had us all get into our positions.

I had to crawl under this pile of garbage they had built. They had put a piece of carpet on the ground for me to lay on and piled up all this crap, leaving a tunnel-like space I would use to crawl in and out of. I was the Oscar-the-Grouch walker. The set guy helping me get into my position told me that he got into the garbage house himself to make sure it was okay. It was just a bit cramped and damp—oh, and there were spiders. He had felt something on his leg while he was in there, and when he got out he realized a spider was crawling up his leg inside his pants. I hate spiders. I was already nervous about my scene, and now I had to worry about spiders

My garbage house filled with spiders. Courtesy Scott Ian.

biting me? I shook it off—walkers don't have arachnophobia, and it was time for me to get into my garbage lair. I crawled in and got into position with my head down and hands pulled in out of sight. The set guy covered up the space in front of me with more garbage, and Greg peeked in and asked, "Are you okay?"

"Hell yeah, never better," I replied.

"You look great in there! You're going to do great," he said, smiling at me. Then Greg gave me direction one last time: "I know it's hard for you to see out from under there, but look for Andrew's leg, and as soon as you see his boot near you, reach out and grab his pants as fast and hard as you can and don't let go—make him yank his leg out of your hand. Cool?"

I said to Greg, "I got it. Let's do it." I was laying there in that dark, wet, and cold space singularly focused on what I had to do, my environment helping me get into a weird place in my mind where I could believe I was a walker. I was able to shut out all the nerves and excitement of actually being in this world I'd watched for so many years and just concentrate on the job at hand: to try to eat Rick and Carl.

Greg yelled, "Action," and I could hear Rick say, "Get ready" to Carl, and then I could hear the sounds of them fighting and I was set, coiled and ready to strike. Rick's leg came into my small field of vision through the garbage, and I thrust forward as fast as I could, grabbing onto his pants and boot as hard as I could. I could feel him yank his leg once, twice, and then on the third try he ripped his leg out of my grasp. I could feel a hot flash of pain from one of my fingers, but I ignored it. I crawled part way out of the hole and kept reaching and growling at Rick and Carl, my single-minded desire to reach them and satiate my appetite for human flesh.

Greg yelled, "Cut," and he walked onto the set, making slight adjustments, giving some direction to Andrew and Chandler. My middle finger on my Rick-grabbing hand was hurting, and I saw that part of my fingernail had been torn off when he pulled his leg away. I was really holding on tight. It was bleeding a bit, and the set guy noticed and asked if I wanted to see the first aid person.

"No, I'm okay. No worries," and in a terrible John Cleese accent I said, "It's just a flesh wound!" Like the Black Knight, I wasn't going to let a tiny little injury mess up my day. Greg came over to me and asked me how I was.

"Fucking great. Do I get to do it again?" I replied, smiling through my walker makeup.

He laughed and said, "Yes, we'll do a few takes and then your close-up. Great job. Oh, you don't have to make any noise, they'll dub in the walker sounds later." I wanted to do my own growls though, as making the sounds helped me feel like a walker, but they weren't going to use them, so I just did them much quieter on the next take. We did two more takes of the same thing, and then it was time for me to die.

Months earlier, when Greg told me I could be a walker on the show, I asked him if I could bite Carl. Yes, I know, it doesn't happen in the comic, but so what? The show had taken its own path many times, differing from

About to break a nail. Courtesy Scott Ian.

what was done in the comic. Why not let me be the walker that takes him down? I would be a hero to all the undead. That one bite would get me into the zombie hall of fame, for sure. Greg just smiled at me as if to say, *Okay, idiot, like that would ever happen in a million years.* And then he said, "I'll figure out a good death for you."

Greg had me crawl further out of my crap pile and had the visual effects (VFX) guy come onto the set to tell me what I needed to do to die like a real *Walking Dead* walker. The plan was for Chandler to slam a "steel" pole (it was rubber) through my head. To do that, my head would need to be in the exact right position to make the effect line up and look great. The VFX guy had a frame, like a template on his screen, and he could see the shot and was able to position my head perfectly so it would match up with Chandler's strike. It was easy when the guy was telling me, "Move left, head up a bit—that's it, don't move, you're perfect."

I was going to have to physically get back to the exact position he framed on my own. Greg explained how to move my head up toward the pole strike, hold it for a second, and then drop quickly to the ground. He had me practice resetting to the position I was in when I was reaching for Andrew and Chandler, and then while Andrew was giving Chandler the steel pole I'd get my upper body and head in position for the pole strike. I didn't have any marks to go by, just feel and hope that I'd line my head up with Chandler's hit. The assistant director yelled, "Quiet on the set!" and in that moment before Greg would yell, "Action!" I was shitting my pants. All my nerves came sizzling back, and all I could think of was that I was going to get this move wrong over and over again and would hold up the whole shoot. I felt like my anxiety was showing through my makeup: Scott Ian as "The Neurotic Walker." *Had they ever fired a walker mid-scene?* I wondered. How the hell was I supposed to get my head in the exact position? I'd never done anything like this before, and then through this whirlpool of stress flooding my brain I heard Greg yell, "Action!" and a switch flipped, and I instantly started growling and clawing at the air in front of me, trying to free myself from my garbage prison so I could get my teeth into some human sushi. Behind my walker façade I heard Carl say his line, "Dad?" asking Rick for the pole so he could dispatch the walker. I watched Rick hand the pole to Carl and made my move into position, hoping for the best. Carl struck downward with the pole, stopping short of my head, and I raised my head upward to meet the pole as directed, holding for a beat and then dropping lifeless. I lay there on the ground as still as I could. I heard someone cheer and then clap from back where Greg watched the scene on a monitor.

Greg yelled, "Cut," and I barely raised my head, not wanting to move too much out of position for the next take.

The set guy came over to me and asked, "Did you hear that cheer after you got killed?"

I quietly said, "Yeah, I did. What's up?"

He told me it was the visual effects guy who cheered and clapped because I hit my mark exactly. The set guy said, "That guy never does that," and he smiled at me and said, "Nice work."

Greg and the VFX guy came over, and the VFX guy said, "You nailed it. The digital pole is going to line up perfectly with your head—good work."

Greg asked me what I thought, and I was all business: "I'm ready to do it again, whatever you need."

A good death. Courtesy Scott Ian.

Greg said, "You're done. You nailed it—you're dead. I told you I'd give you a good death." Greg helped me up and said, "Good work, buddy! You're a natural!" We hugged and then he went back to work.

I just stood there for a minute in a daze as everyone on set buzzed around me, doing their thing, getting ready for the next shot. I was ecstatic about being a part of the show and doing a good job, and I was sad to be done. It went by so fast—so much foreplay and then bang, finished. A production assistant came over and asked if I wanted to go get the makeup taken off, but I still had stuff to do for the *Bloodworks* episode, so at least I could keep the makeup on for a little while longer. I wasn't ready to let go of my walker.

I did some on-camera interview segments for *Bloodworks* and then did a photo shoot with Andrew and Chandler. They were both very cool, and it turns out Andrew is a Motörhead fan, so I told him my Lemmy pants-full-of-poo-fighting-a-Nazi drinking story (as told in my book *I'm the Man*). They both got a kick out of that tale. Greg had a short break after I was done with Andrew and Chandler, and we got to take some pictures and talk for a few minutes. I must've thanked Greg a hundred times for making the whole thing happen for me. It was truly one of the coolest experiences of my life, and he's the man who enabled it. Greg

Happier times with Chandler and Andrew. Courtesy Scott Ian.

had to get back to directing, and I was taken to the catering tent for lunch. I noticed that all the actors playing walkers ate with their makeup on, so I did the same. I was one of them now.

I flew home the next day and spent the next few weeks looking at my pictures from the set. Until we got the green light from AMC we were under strict orders to keep quiet. It was hard for me to not talk about it—I was bursting. I wanted to shout it out in the street: "I got to be a walker on *The Walking Dead,* motherfuckers!!!" I'd hear from Greg every few weeks, telling me the scene looked great and that I was going to be very happy. Jack was busy cutting together the *Bloodworks* episode, so it would be ready for whenever AMC said we could air it. Finally they did. *The Walking Dead* would air season five, episode twelve, now titled "Remember," on March 1, 2015.

I watched the episode with my wife at home and waited nervously for my scene. At thirty-four minutes and eleven seconds into the show I made my cable television debut as a walker. The ratings say 14.43 million people watched the episode in the United States, up a million viewers from the week before. You're welcome.

The whole scene from when I grab Rick's pants to getting impaled is only twenty seconds, but for me it's a lifelong dream realized.

And Greg gave me a great death.

Afterword

Our *Bloodworks/The Walking Dead* episode quickly became the most-watched episode we'd ever done. It was huge. Go check it out at Nerdist.com.

On the episode of *Talking Dead* that aired that night they showed a picture of my walker in the "In Memoriam" segment and named it "Steel Pole Head Walker."

The nerd-me loves that I am on *The Walking Dead* IMDB page for this episode as an "uncredited walker."

Okay, I just looked at the clock on my laptop and saw that it is now 12:49 a.m. on March 1, 2017. It's two years to the day when my episode aired, and I am finishing this story. That is a trip!

It's been two years, and I still get asked almost every day in interviews or by people who recognize me in the street: "What was it like to be on *The Walking Dead?*" And I always answer, "It was the best ever."

My Belushi ghost-hunting partner Greg Nicotero.
Thank you for making this possible! Courtesy Scott Ian.

THAT'S NOT A ROCK

RING. RING. RRRRIIIINNNNGGGG.

The phone was ringing way too early in the morning after a late-night recording session.

"Who the hell," I mumbled as I rolled over to answer. "Hello. Hello?"

Click.

Fucking hell.

I rolled back over to go back to sleep and

RING. RRRRRRRRING.

"Fuck it," I thought. I let the machine get it and closed my eyes to go back to sleep.

"Hey Scott. It's Bryan. Don't come to the studio today. There was a flood. All right, talk to you later."

Click.

Now I was awake.

It was January 1993, and we were in Los Angeles recording *Sound of White Noise* at Eldorado Studios with Dave Jerden producing. The caller was our engineer, Bryan Carlstrom (RIP).

A flood? It had been raining a lot, every day for two weeks straight. But a flood? In the studio? Did the two-inch masters get damaged? Is our album ruined? What about my guitars? I was in the middle of tracking my rhythm guitars at this point and had guitars on stands all over the studio. Fuck.

Bryan didn't give any details in his message, so I grabbed the phone and called right back. Bryan answered, and even before I could ask a question he told me the tapes were okay. That was a relief. The idea of having to retrack all the drums and most of my guitars was a nightmare. Then he told me all my guitars were fine. They were all in the live room, and the flood was only in the control room, specifically right over the board. The ceiling had collapsed at some point overnight, and dry wall, acoustic tiling crap, and a whole lot of water slammed down into the console. It was fried.

"Holy crap" was all I could muster. "What are we going to do?"

We were only about 25 percent done with what was quite an important record for us—our first with John Bush on vocals—and we couldn't just stop everything and remain in some holding pattern, waiting to finish. It'd blow all the vibe and momentum we had been building over the previous months.

"Dave has been on the phone all morning trying to find another studio with time available. We're hoping to get your gear out of here today and over to another spot so we can fire up and start getting tones in another room tomorrow," Bryan said confidently. We were in Los Angeles, where there's no shortage of great rooms. "So what happened? Do you know why it flooded?" I asked. "No idea yet. I'll keep you posted," he replied.

I went back to bed. It felt like a snow day at school. On the upside: an unexpected day off!

I got a call later that day from Dave, and he told me we were all set to go at the legendary Cherokee Studios in Hollywood the next day. I was really excited, as they had made some great records there, from David Bowie to Frank Sinatra to Michael Jackson.

I told Dave I was really sorry and that I couldn't believe what had happened at Eldorado and couldn't imagine what a hassle it was going to be to get that control room cleaned up and the board fixed. Dave was one of the owners of the studio, and it was on him. He told me he couldn't understand why the ceiling would've flooded like that, so he climbed up onto the roof of the studio to take a look. The building was an old two story that had a four-foot-high wall around the roof. Dave saw that the roof had basically turned into a lake. It had filled with water, at least three feet deep. It hadn't all caved in into the control room, just a portion below. He was lucky: if the whole thing had gone to shit, the studio would've been destroyed along with our record and gear.

He got some hip-wader boots and gloves and walked out across the roof toward one of the corners where there was a drain. He reached into the drain and started pulling out all kinds of crap—leaves and twigs, garbage, and so on—and then his hand touched something solid and hard like a rock. He figured he'd found the reason the drain clogged and all the water backed up. He pulled at the rock, dislodging it from the drain, and when he pulled it out from the water he saw that it wasn't a rock.

It was a skull. A dog's skull.

Dave was very confused. A dog's skull? How the fuck did that get into the drain? Did a dog get left on the roof at some point and die there? If so where were the rest of the bones? And how the hell would a dog have gotten left on the roof? Did some nut-job walking past the studio on Sunset Boulevard throw a dog's skull up onto the roof, where it eventually made its way into the drain? There were a lot of freaks hanging around that area of Sunset back then. Did someone sacrifice a dog in some weird ritual? So many questions and no answers. It was a real mystery.

Dave and I were talking about this, going over all these scenarios, when I remembered that he had produced the Jane's Addiction record *Ritual de lo Habitual* and had told me that some vocals had been recorded at Eldorado. The song "Been Caught Stealing" is on that record, and there's a dog barking in the background in the intro to the song. I had asked Dave about the dog barking weeks earlier and how they recorded that, and he told me that the barking dog ran into the studio while they were recording and they decided to keep it on the track.

A disturbing light bulb went off in my brain. Did Jane's Addiction kill that dog? Was that the Ritual de lo Habitual?

"Dave, is that the dog from 'Been Caught Stealing'?"

Dave didn't answer right away, and I thought, *Holy crap, it is that dog! Jesus. What the fuck is up with that?* I had heard those guys were weird, but this was fucking crazy shit.

Then Dave started laughing. *Is he fucking with me?* I thought. Dave was a great ballbuster.

Finally Dave said, "No, Scott, it's not. I wish I could say it was. What a story that would be! Anyway, the skull is not big enough to have been that dog."

And that was that.

We finished the record and the rest is history.

Except for that skull.

ALL-IN

Part Two

I woke up on Friday, April 15, 2011, smiling. I had a lot to smile about. It was Pearl's birthday, and she was just about seven months pregnant and doing great. We had plans to celebrate that evening with friends. I kissed Pearl good morning and serenaded her with a pre-coffee-gravel-voiced rendition of "Happy Birthday." It was a beautiful Los Angeles day, and I got out of bed to make coffee. I wasn't on tour at the time—Anthrax was still working on the *Worship Music* album—so my daily schedule was very relaxed: breakfast and then sign on to Ultimate Bet to play some poker before going on a hike with Pearl, running errands, and so on. At this point I had been playing online professionally for Ultimate Bet for three years, and poker had become a major part of my life.

When I was home I'd play online thirty to forty hours a week, multitabling $100 and $200 no-limit hold 'em Sit & Go Turbos (six seated tournaments where the blinds go up very quickly). Those tournaments were my specialty, and I'd play up to ten tables at a time. If I was touring, I'd play sixty to seventy hours a week. Poker had become a great way to kill time on tour and was very lucrative. Playing online had become an ATM for me, and I had just signed a new two-year deal with Ultimate Bet to continue being one of their pros. That meant they pay me to play poker on their site, they pay for my tournament buy-ins, and I get to keep the winnings. Yes, you read that right: I wasn't playing with my own money. It was pretty much the best job ever. Until it wasn't.

I took my coffee into our office and turned on my Mac and the big-screen monitor that my buddy Dixon, a poker-whiz who also played on Ultimate Bet, so kindly gave me for a birthday present so I could multitable in style instead of squinting at a bunch of tiny tables on my laptop. I signed into Ultimate Bet like I had done for the last three years and immediately knew something was very wrong because this window popped open on my screen:

This domain name has been seized by the F.B.I. pursuant to an Arrest Warrant in Rem obtained by the United States Attorney's Office for the Southern District of New York and issued by the United States District Court for the Southern District of New York.

Conducting, financing, managing, supervising, directing, or owning all or part of an illegal gambling business is a federal crime. (18 U.S.C. § 1955)

For persons engaged in the business of betting or wagering, it is also a federal crime to knowingly accept, in connection with the participation of another person in unlawful Internet gambling, credit, electronic fund transfers, or checks. (31 U.S.C. § § 5363 & 5366)

Violations of these laws carry criminal penalties of up to five years' imprisonment and a fine of up to $250,000.

Properties, including domain names, used in violation of the provisions of 18 U.S.C. § 1955 or involved in money laundering transactions are subject to forfeiture to the United States. (18 U.S.C. § § 981 & 1955(d))

"Um, what the fuck? WHAT THE FUCK?"

Pearl heard me yell and came into the office to see what was happening. I was standing there stunned, just pointing at the screen like Donald Sutherland at the end of *Invasion of the Body Snatchers.*

At first glance I thought the Department of Justice was coming to arrest me. I slowed down and read it carefully and still thought that somehow I was in trouble. Had anyone else got this window? I tried to close the window but couldn't. I shut down my computer, restarted, and immediately started emailing my fellow poker players.

It wasn't just me.

The US Department of Justice had seized the dot-com Internet addresses of PokerStars, Full Tilt Poker, and Cereus (Ultimate Bet and Absolute Poker), among others. The US government had a federal criminal case charging the defendants with violating the Unlawful Internet Gambling Enforcement Act (UIGEA) of 2006 alleging that they engaged in bank fraud and money laundering to process transfers to and from their customers. Here's a quick layman's terms history of the UIGEA:

UIGEA is an antigambling law that passed Congress on September 30, 2006. President George W. Bush signed it into law on October 13, 2006. In my not-so-humble opinion the UIGEA is bullshit. The bill was attached to another bill, the Safe Port Act of 2006, which was a counter-terrorism bill that created funding to secure our ports. Everyone wants that, right? Even though the two bills are completely unrelated, the UIGEA was attached without debate. No one read it, no one cared because we want safe ports, and in an eleventh-hour vote before the 2006 election recess Congress pretty much unanimously voted for this bill without ever reading the UIGEA. Hey, they were fighting terrorism and had vacation plans—there's no time to actually read what they were voting on. Many US senators who voted for this bill didn't even know the UIGEA was attached. The UIGEA didn't make anything new illegal. What it did was add a layer of enforcement against individuals and companies processing payments for illegal Internet gambling.

Unregulated Internet gambling had exploded in 2003 because of the "Moneymaker effect." Back in 2003 Chris Moneymaker (yes, that is his real name), an accountant from Tennessee, qualified for the World Series of Poker Main Event on a then relatively unknown online poker site called PokerStars. He bought into a satellite event, an eighteen-person tournament for $39, and won it. That advanced him into a $600 satellite tournament that had 68 players and awarded World Series of Poker Main Event seats to the top three spots. He won his $10,000 Main Event seat, and to the surprise of everyone, Moneymaker maneuvered his way through a shark-infested field of 839 players to win the Main Event and its $2.5 million first-place prize. It was Moneymaker's first live poker tournament. The aptly named Moneymaker was an everyman, the kind of guy you'd like to have a beer with, and people related to his story in a huge way. The publicity surrounding his win was massive; he even appeared on the *Tonight Show* with Jay Leno, and the coverage on ESPN was relentless because they were dealing with the 2004–2005 NHL lockout and needed programming. Moneymaker's fairytale story was ratings gold. In the years that followed his win the attendance for the Main Event jumped from 839 in 2003 to 8,773 in 2006. The "Moneymaker effect" led millions of people who thought they could be "just like Chris" to online poker rooms. The poker boom was born.

In the years leading up to the passage of the UIGEA in 2006 online poker operated in a gray area of the law. It was already unlawful to process payments, but the UIGEA created additional punishment for those found guilty of doing so. The online gaming companies that stayed in business in the United States post-UIGEA moved offshore and kept offering real-money play in direct conflict with the new law. They were practically flaunting the fact that they were making billions of dollars. Online poker was all over our TV sets, sponsoring the numerous poker shows that popped up during the poker boom. Even major networks like NBC, who had the annual National Heads Up Poker Championship and Poker After Dark, were reaping the benefits of online poker dollars from all the advertising they would buy on those shows. Every commercial was for an online site. The World Series of Poker was now regular programming on ESPN, attracting tens of thousands of players from all over the world and millions of viewers. There were poker magazines all over the newsstands; poker players like Phil Hellmuth, Daniel Negreanu, Phil Ivey, and Chris Ferguson were like the new rock stars. Everyone wanted to be like and hang with them. Poker was booming; it was a modern-day gold rush and all in the face of the US government, which wasn't getting their piece of the action. This went on until April 15, 2011, the day that would become known as Black Friday for online poker. The government shut it all down. They didn't even try to regulate it and tax it, missing out on billions in tax dollars. They just shut it down, making it illegal and impossible for US players to play online and taking away people's jobs and livelihoods.

I sat there dejectedly staring at the Department of Justice message on my screen. In three years I had gone from less than a rank amateur to a sponsored pro. How the hell had I got here? How did I go from luckily beating Sully on VH1 Classic to cashing in the Main Event of the World Series of Poker myself? Let's go back to 2006.

In the wake of winning the *VH1 Classic Rock and Roll Celebrity Poker Tournament,* I forgot all about it. As exciting as the whole thing was, I wasn't a poker player. I didn't start playing after that win because I was busy writing a record at the time. Months went by, and then the tournament aired on VH1 Classic in March of 2007. I got hit up to do some interviews about winning, and I just played it off as beginner's luck. Again, I really didn't care; it was just some innocent fun in Vegas. The week after the tournament aired I got a phone call at home. I wasn't really paying attention when the woman on the line told me her name and why she was calling. All I heard was something about Aruba. I said, "Excuse me, sorry, I missed what you were saying."

She repeated, "Hi Scott. My name is Joanne Priam, and I am from Ultimate Bet. I am calling you to help make your arrangements for your trip to Aruba to play in our tournament there September 29 through October 6."

I muttered something like, "Huh, um, okay, what is this for? A trip to Aruba?" I had no memory of winning anything. I only remembered the big check that went to charity.

Joanne said, "Yes, you won a trip to Aruba and a seat in our $5,000 buy-in tournament." Things became a bit clearer.

I replied, "Ah, okay. When is it again?" I figured I wouldn't be able to go—I'm always busy with the band. She told me again when the trip was, and I checked my schedule. I didn't have anything scheduled for the end of September to the beginning of October—granted, it was six months out. I told Joanne I was free and asked if I could bring Pearl.

She said, "Of course! It's a trip for two." Joanne only had good answers.

I asked her to hold on and told Pearl what was happening. "Do you want to go to Aruba for a week and hang out with a bunch of poker players?"

Always game for an adventure, Pearl smiled and said, "Yeah, sounds like fun." I told Joanne we were in. It's weird how one innocuous phone call can change your whole life.

Six months later we were on our way to Aruba. I was going to be playing in Ultimate Bet's big tournament, so I did practice a little bit leading up to the trip. Mostly I watched poker on TV. I was going to be getting lessons and tips from Phil Hellmuth and some of the Ultimate Bet online pros like Gary "debo34" DeBernardi, Mark "PokerHo" Kroon, and Wisco Murray as well. That was the beginning of my real poker education.

I spent a week playing with Phil and the guys, absorbing as much as I could. It didn't help that I managed to bust out of the

Pearl and me in Aruba with Phil Hellmuth,
waiting for the vintage Dom to chill. Courtesy Scott Ian.

My mentors! Left to right: Mark "PokerHo" Kroon, Will Griffiths,
Phil Hellmuth, me, and Gary "debo34" DeBernardi. Courtesy Scott Ian.

main event in Aruba on day one, set over set, meaning my three
jacks lost to the other guy's three kings. I wasn't angry about it;
there was nothing I could do. I wasn't folding. Pearl and I got to
spend the rest of the week on the beach during the day and raging with our new poker friends at night. RAGING. Party like a

rock star? Nope. Party like a poker player. These people partied like band dudes did in the 1980s. And on top of the booze and drugs, they would bet on anything. They would bet on how many ice cubes were going to be in someone's drink. They would bet on who would get served first at meals. They would play credit card roulette at the end of a meal, where everyone puts their card in a pile and the card that gets picked pays for the whole dinner. This could get very pricey, as these guys were all ordering steaks and bottles of vintage wine and champagne. Then there were the prop (proposition) bets. I don't know if poker players get bored at the table while they are playing or just crave action so much that they need to find their fix no matter how ridiculous the bet. My new friends told me stories about a $2 million weight loss bet where the guy had to lose 48 pounds in three months. He had to go from 188 pounds to under 140. And he did it, ending up at 138 pounds. A six-figure bet where a guy had to move to casino-free Des Moines, Iowa, for thirty days. He lasted two. A $50,000 bet on whether a guy could stand in the ocean (he could wear a wetsuit) for twenty-four hours. He lasted three hours. How about $10,000 for a strict vegetarian to eat a cheeseburger? He ate it and didn't even get a stomachache. There was a six-figure bet to see if a guy could live in the bathroom of his room at the Bellagio Hotel for thirty days. He couldn't leave the bathroom at any time and his access to food, a DVD player, and talking on the phone were strictly limited. The guy was doing so well at living in the bathroom that they settled on ending the bet early for $40,000. Or how about a $300,000 bet on whether a guy could run seventy miles on a treadmill in twenty-four hours? Could you do that? I couldn't. The guy did it in twenty-three hours and fifteen minutes. These prop bets were a window into the degenerate nature of real gamblers. There was nothing they wouldn't wager on. I had guys offering me money to shave my goatee. I set a price of $100,000. One guy offered me $99,000, saying, "If you'll do it for $100,000, you'll do it for $99,000." I called his bluff. He smiled and walked away.

Who can keep at least one hand out of the water the longest
for $10,000? My money is on Joanne!
Left to right: Phil Hellmuth, me, Liv Boeree, Joanne Priam,
Adam Levy, and PokerHo in Aruba. Courtesy Scott Ian.

I had a great week hanging out in the poker world for the first time. The energy was fantastic, and I made some interesting new friends. A few weeks after Aruba I got another call, this time from their head of marketing, a tall bald English gentleman named Will Griffiths. I had met Will in Aruba, and we hit it off immediately. We caught up, and then Will said, "So mate, we'd like to sign you up as one of our pro players."

This seemed ridiculous to me, so I said, "Me? I'm terrible at poker."

Will said dryly, "We're not signing you for your poker prowess, mate. It's because of who you are and your potential to bring in a lot of new players. We can run tournaments and advertise that people can play with you and chat with you and they get a bonus if they knock you out."

This I understood. "Ah, okay, I get it," I said. "I am definitely interested. But if I do this, I want poker lessons. I want to really learn how to play and not just be some donkey celebrity." (Donkey was a derogatory term in the poker world for a shit player.)

Will said they could make that a part of my deal. "Who do you want to take lessons from?" he asked.

I was friends with Phil Hellmuth and thought we'd be a good match, but Phil lived up in Northern California and it'd be tough to make that work. I had met Annie Duke, a poker pro and one of Ultimate Bet's real sponsored professionals in Aruba. Annie was cool, and her math-based approach to poker was right up my alley, as I've always had a math brain and she lived in Los Angeles. I knew that Annie had given lessons to Ben Affleck, and he went on to win the California State Poker Championship in 2004. I told Will, "I want lessons with Annie."

Will said, "No worries, mate. Consider it done."

I got all signed up with Ultimate Bet (I'm going to abbreviate it UB) and started playing online as much as I could. I loved playing—it was a lot of fun to meet people online and chat with them at the tables. The players on UB seemed happy that I was a part of the site and that I was into poker. I'm sure they also liked that I wasn't very good and easy to play against. I was getting an education on UB's dime. I was playing with their money. Essentially it was no-risk gambling, which made it easier for me to learn how to play, knowing I wasn't risking my mortgage.

Once I started my lessons with Annie it all changed. One of the first things I learned was that poker is not gambling. If you learn the math, there is a mathematical edge, and over time you will win more than you lose. Why do you think you see the same pros

I'm a poker pro! You can tell by how well I am tossing those chips. Courtesy Scott Ian.

winning all the time? It is a game of skill. My lessons with Annie combined with my grinding hours online developing my game turned me into a poker player, and I started to see the results. I was starting to win. I took to no-limit hold 'em, and I committed. As they say, I was all in. I was as focused and determined with the same intense drive to succeed at poker as I was about making my band succeed in the early days of Anthrax, the same force of will to make things happen and accept nothing but success. The odds of starting a band and making it in the music business are astronomical—I'll let Annie Duke figure those out. Accomplishing that insane task gave me the, for lack of a better word, balls to know that I could be a successful poker player.

I dove in and became a fixture on the site. I played constantly, sometimes as much as eighty hours a week when I was on tour. I was literally playing on stage during sound checks. I'd be playing guitar with one hand and raising/folding with the other. I'll bet $100,000 that I'm the only person who has done that kind of multitasking. Sometimes I'd give my guitar tech instructions on hands to play if I knew I wouldn't be able to play for a few minutes. I was playing in the dressing room all day long. I was playing on the bus

Wi-Fi on our overnight drives. I was playing in the recording studio while we were making The Damned Things album *Ironiclast* and the Anthrax album *Worship Music.* If you read the lyrics to The Damned Things' song "A Great Reckoning," you'll hear Keith sing some of my poker-inspired words: "King gets his aces cracked ..." And the Anthrax songs "The Devil You Know" and "Crawl" are all about the emotional roller coaster of playing no-limit hold 'em. I was always playing.

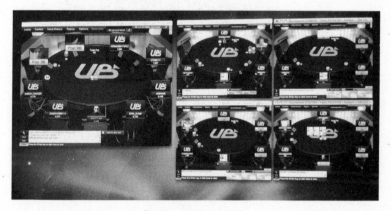

Grinding away! Courtesy Scott Ian.

UB had their big weekly $200,000 guaranteed tournament every Sunday. Guaranteed meant that no matter how many people entered the tourney, they would pay out $200,000 in prize money. It cost $200 to buy in to the tourney, and most of the time there were over a thousand entries, so UB didn't need to overlay to cover it. I played that tourney every Sunday. As one of the pros, I had a bounty on me, so if you knocked me out of the tourney, you'd get your buy-in back. Players were happy to have me at their table so they could try to bust me and receive their reward. I found that it would make players play looser against me, and I used that to my advantage, knowing their range of hands would be bigger than normal. More times than not, if I would get all my chips in, I would have the better starting hand, and then I would just hope it would hold up. When you have the stronger starting hand and you lose to a weaker starting hand, that is called a bad beat. Here's an example:

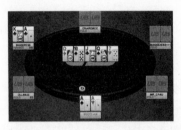

Cracked! One of the many joys of poker. Courtesy Scott Ian.

At the start of this hand, preflop I am an 87.6 percent favorite to win the hand. Then the player I am against flops a straight and cracks my aces. That is a bad beat. Worse (because the odds would be even lower for him to win it) would be if he didn't flop the straight and made it on the river, the last card dealt where his only out (card that makes his hand a winner) would be the card he needed to make the straight. Either way, this scenario is known as a suck-out. Bad beats are a part of the game, and when you're playing so many hands online (online moves much faster than playing live poker) you're going to have your share of them. I learned early on to not dwell on these seemingly bad-luck or "cooler" hands and just move forward.

Throughout 2008 I learned everything I could about hold 'em. I had my lessons with Annie, I was reading poker books, and I was playing constantly, absorbing everything I could and putting my knowledge into action and learning from my mistakes. Poker had become my priority. I was starting to win money consistently in the sit-and-go tournaments I played. I was starting to finish higher in the big Sunday tournament, cashing it (the top 10 percent got paid, so if there were 1,200 entries, usually around the top 120 got paid) pretty regularly. Then in March 2009 things got real.

I wasn't even supposed to play the $200,000 tourney on Sunday, March 29, 2009. I was supposed to be in Scottsdale, Arizona, for my aunt and uncle's surprise anniversary party. I was feeling sick on Friday, feverish like a flu was coming on, so Pearl and I decided to wait and see how I felt the next day and then we'd decide whether we were going to drive to Scottsdale for the party. I woke up Saturday feeling even worse, so we had to cancel our trip. On Sunday morning I was still sick, with a 102-degree fever with chills, achy—the whole shit-show. The Sunday $200,000 was starting, and I decided that, as I was just laying on the couch and all I had to do was push some computer keys to play, I would buy in and play the tournament. I figured I would bust out quickly, as I was feeling so crappy and my decision-making skills would be dulled. Eight hours later I was at the final table with a big stack of chips and gunning for the win. My adrenaline was running so strong that any vestige of flu was pushed to the side as I vied for the tournament victory. It got down to heads-up, and I won it. I stood up from the couch in silence. Pearl asked me if I was okay, and I told her, "I just won. I just won it. Holy crap, I did it." I had outlasted 1,007 runners (players) to win my first big tournament. I cashed for $44,000 and change, and I sat back down as the flu came crashing back in as my adrenaline surge waned.

Winning that tourney was a big deal for me. It put me on the map as a real player and showed the people at UB that I was taking this very seriously and that their investment in me was a good one. Winning it wasn't a fluke; I had cashed the $200,000 many times, even finishing in the top ten three times—ninth, seventh, and fourth—and landing five or six times in the top twenty. And every time I would bust out, especially the time I finished in fourth place, I would think, *How the hell do you win this? I got this far only to blow it.* I had just accomplished the seemingly impossible, and winning only pushed me to work even harder at my game.

Straddling two worlds was becoming difficult. Anthrax and poker were crossing over into one another, and the lack of down time was starting to take a toll on me as well as those around me. I was always working, usually in both worlds at the same time. Either one of these jobs is a 24/7 gig, and I was doing both. My focus was certainly being blurred, and that was affecting Anthrax. For the band 2009 was a transition period; we were writing songs for what would become *Worship Music,* and we were trying to move ahead with a new singer, slowly moving forward, playing some shows here and there but with no real tour schedule. I was very excited about the songs we were working on, but everything else band business–wise was like pulling teeth trying to get back on our feet and be seen as a viable commodity in the metal world. In that moment Anthrax was a struggle, a constant battle for us to remain afloat, and I fought that fight every day no matter what. I would never walk away from my band. But poker became my escape from the music business. I was still in the honeymoon phase with poker, and playing was satisfying me in the same way playing music did. Poker gave me the energy to keep moving forward and was also paying the bills, which was a huge help.

The 2009 World Series of Poker (WSOP) was looming on my horizon. The WSOP runs from the end of May until mid-July every summer, and that's primetime-touring season as well, so it's hard for me to be able to play in it. I had tried to play some events in 2008, but my schedule wouldn't allow for it. Going into the 2009 WSOP I made sure I'd be able to play some of the smaller buy-in tourneys and was hoping to play the $10,000 buy-in main event. When I compared my band schedule to the WSOP main event dates I thought someone was fucking with me: it was as if the metal and poker gods got in a room to discuss my schedule and made a prop bet to see if I would be able to handle what it would take schedule-wise to play the main event. They would align all the planets so I could play but with a catch: my schedule would be so impossible that I couldn't possibly make it, let alone cash or win. Anthrax was on tour in Europe in June, and we'd be finishing our tour the day before the last day one that the main event was scheduled to start. They need to have four starting days—1A, 1B, 1C, 1D—to accommodate all the players who want to play the main event just to fit them into all the card rooms set up at the Rio Hotel and Casino. I was going to make day 1D by the skin of my teeth.

I got to Las Vegas from Germany on Sunday, July 5. We had just completed a three-week tour playing the Sonisphere festivals with Metallica all over Europe, and I was happy about the shows we'd played but also very tired. I got to Vegas at 8 p.m., dropped my bags at the Hard Rock Hotel, and headed straight for the Rio (home of the WSOP) to buy in to the main event. I decided to buy in the night before because I knew that if I waited to buy in the morning of day 1D, I would be fucked. I was right. The next morning the lines were crazy, filled with people trying to get into the last main event starting day at the last minute, and people got shut out because it was over capacity. I had just traveled fifteen hours and got my ass to the Rio as soon as I got to Vegas to claim my seat, so I have no sympathy for anyone who waited until the morning of and got denied. I got to bed by midnight with jet lag and all my excitement to play the main event wrestling with each other. I lay there until finally my body just took control and told my brain to not be an asshole and let me sleep.

I got to the Rio Monday morning at 11 a.m. for day 1D. I made it. I stood there in the hallway for a few minutes, taking it all in. I was right in the middle of poker's biggest party, and the vibe was incredible: 6,494 people had bought in to play the main event, and we all thought we could win it. I was excited, like jumping-out-of-my-skin excited. I had a coffee in the Ultimate Bet suite and was off to find my seat. I was so adrenalized about playing that I barely felt my feet touching the floor as I walked to my table. Day 1D was a five-level (two-hour levels, blinds go up each level, with a thirty-minute break between levels) blur of intensity and focus. I got dealt AA midway through the day and fired every street (betting the flop, turn, and river) on a Qd6d6s4d3s board. I bet $7,000 on the river, and the guy went into the tank (making his decision on what to do) for three minutes. He finally called and mucked (folded) like Quicksilver when I showed AA. That got me to over $40,000 in chips. I could've played five more levels if I had to, I was so amped to be there. I ended up with an above-average chip stack at the end of the night and was looking forward to the day off while they played day 2A of the main event the next day. A side note to that: I had asked about playing day 2A instead of 2B because of my crazy schedule and was even able to personally ask the head of the WSOP, Jeff Pollack, about it, but it wasn't going to happen.

I spent Tuesday doing nothing. Literally. I slept twenty hours recovering from my flight in from Europe and the tour. I was mentally and physically preparing for the monster I was going to need to beat in order to make it through the week.

I played day 2B on Wednesday, and once again I played my game, staying focused and patient. It paid off, as late in the day I found myself with AA again with another player all-in preflop and another player in the pot. With about $40,000 in the pot, the flop came 8d6d3d. I bet $13,000, and the other player folded. I turn over AcAd. The all-in guy had QsJh. The turn and river come 7s5c, and I chipped up to $106,000. After that things got tough, and over the next level of play I was slowly draining chips, card-dead forever. I stayed scrappy and was in okay shape by the end of it.

The day finished at 1:30 a.m., and I had a little less than the tourney average chip stack. I felt okay about my play and had made it to day three. At this point over half the field had been eliminated, and I was still in it, so I was happy. I bagged up my chips and ran to grab a taxi back to my hotel, where I would shower, sleep two hours, and get back into a taxi to the airport at 4:30 a.m. to make my flight to Tulsa.

What the hell did you just say? Where the hell are you going in the middle of the main event? Why are you going to Tulsa?

Remember the catch I was talking about earlier?

Anthrax had a festival to play in Tulsa, Oklahoma, on Thursday, July 9, which was the media day of the main event, so no tourney that day, so I had the day off. Knowing for months that I would be able to play the main, arriving from Europe hours before day 1D and with this one show right in the middle of it didn't make it any easier for me now that I was here. The only thing keeping me going was the adrenaline and excitement of being able to be there playing hold 'em in the main event. And if I were to make it to the final nine players at the end of the main event, I had to fly out the next day to Sweden to continue the tour. It was a perfect yet insane window of time. I was doing everything in my power to not fuck it up.

I barely slept and got to the deserted airport at 4:30 a.m. No one was leaving Las Vegas in the middle of the main event except me. I was a zombie. I flew at 6 a.m. from Las Vegas, with a stop in Denver, and then on to Tulsa, arriving at 2 p.m. I slept on the flight and headed straight out to the festival site, which was an hour drive away. We were headlining the opening night of the Rocklahoma festival. I was already dreading the fact that we were going to be off stage after midnight and then I had an hour drive back to the hotel, shower, no sleep, and back to the airport by 4:30 a.m. so I could make it back to the Rio by noon on Friday for day three of the tourney. This scenario actually frightened me. How was I physically going to pull this off?

The show was killer, the crowd was awesome, and I stored that energy in my reserve tank to help me make it through the next twenty-four hours. I made it to the Tulsa airport in time for my flight back to Vegas, and even my connecting flight through Denver was on time. I thought for sure there would be a delay and I would be sitting in the Denver airport waiting for my Vegas flight as I got blinded off (if you don't show up to your seat, the dealer will place your blinds for you each round and fold your hand) to nothing. Nope. No way. I was on a mission, and I was going to make it. And not only did I make it, but the flight was even fifteen minutes early so I was able to check back into my hotel, shower, and make the Rio by 11:15 a.m., forty-five minutes before the start of day three. The poker gods were watching over me. I am sure I am the only person at the Rio who flew out and played a show the night before day three. I wish someone had bet me that I couldn't do it. I started mainlining coffee and headed into the tournament room.

I was feeling pretty good, all things considered, totally pumped about making day three. I'm usually quiet at the table when I am playing poker, maybe some small talk once in a while, but today I started out all talk. I was telling some people who recognized me at my table all about my trip to Tulsa. They couldn't believe I had done all that and made it back to play. Just being there gave me confidence.

Day three was tough. I lost a couple of pots early on and was in the thirty BB (big blind) range. No need to panic yet, but I was feeling the stress of the week, and that was letting the pressure get to me. It was hard to stay patient. I was playing aggressively, trying to chip up, but I was card-dead for well over a whole level, and it was hard to stay engaged while having to fold every hand because there was no stealing at my table. Someone was always calling or re-raising. I had enough chips to raise/fold maybe twice if I wanted to try to steal. I calmed myself down and just kept folding all the crap hands and did my best to stay in my game. *Patience, my son. Stay focused on your goal.* Like Quint hunting that shark, I was going to make it to day four. Finally UTG (under the gun, the position at the table that is the first to act preflop) raises to $3,000, and I re-raise with AcQc from the button to $7,500. He calls. The flop comes Kd9d2s. He checks, I bet $13,500, and he folds. Finally a little breathing room. The rest of the day went okay, and I was going to day four with $152,000, a little under average stack but playable, for sure. I barely remember getting in a taxi from the Rio back to the Palazzo. I crashed hard that night.

I was back for day four, still pretty burnt but definitely energized by the fact that the bubble (the point in a tournament when the next player out doesn't make the money but everyone after that player is in the money) would break. I only got involved in one questionable hand about twenty people from the money. Middle position raiser makes it $11,000. I re-raise from the BB with AK to $30,000. The guy shoves (goes all-in) and has me covered. I have $120,000 behind (left in my chip stack). I think about it for two minutes and decide to fold. I'd seen this guy play only two other hands, AA and QQ. He was playing very tight, meaning he must have a big hand in this spot. I wasn't going to coin-flip for my tournament life that close to the money. When I folded I showed my cards, and he turned over A10. I had him crushed. I was kicking myself, but later that day I was okay with the fold. If I call and he spikes a 10, I'd still be crazy over it, really crazy, like pants-full-of-poo, fighting-a-ghost crazy. That's a bad beat I wouldn't be able to just walk away from.

The tourney finally got to hand-for-hand play—when all the tables need to have hands dealt at the same time so you could finish a hand at your table and then have to sit there and wait five minutes until all the tables in the room finish their hands so the tournament director will know for sure who the last player is before the tournament goes into the money.

Hand-for-hand took forever, the pace slowed to a crawl, and then finally the bubble burst. We were in the money! A big cheer went up all across the room as the 680 or so players left all cashed. I have to admit that I was really excited about making the money. My first main event, and I cashed! I was more excited for this than I was for winning the UB $200,000 tourney. This was four days of excruciating mental and physical exertion to stay focused and, on top of that, the challenge of all the travel in the middle of it. My mind was blown.

My table broke (split up) right after the bubble, which was a bummer because now I'd have to deal with eight new players. On top of that, my own bubble had burst as well, and I could feel the whole crazy week pulling me down like hungry zombies (aren't all zombies hungry?). I'd lost my focus and was just hoping to make the next break between levels so I could get my head together and regroup. I kept my head in the game as well as I could at that point and then got into a hand. I had J7 in the BB (the blinds were up to $3,000/$6,000 now). The SB (small blind) limped (just calls), and I checked. Flop comes 10-7-2 rainbow (three different suits). He bets $6,500. I think he's lying and just trying to steal the pot, and I paired my 7, so I re-raise to $17,500 with $59,000 behind. He shoves. Ugh. What do I do now? I can fold and still have just under ten big blinds. That's enough to play, hopefully double up quickly and make it through day four. That would've been the right play, but I'd lost my focus. I was tired, and with that, I'd lost my patience and I called. He turns over AA, and I am gut-punched. A 9 came on the turn, increasing my outs with the gut-shot straight draw. Would I hit on the river, a miracle suck-out to double me up and keep my hopes of winning the WSOP main event alive?

The 4 on the river brought me back to earth, and I was out. With a huge exhale, I got up from the table and headed to the cashier. I placed 637th out of 6,494 and cashed for $21,365, and I'm stoked. I walked out of the Rio a smiley-faced winner and can't wait to do it again without an Anthrax show right in the middle of it. First thing I did was call Pearl to tell her I'd be home the next day. We'd been apart for four weeks at that point, and I couldn't wait to see my lady. She was very excited about me cashing my first WSOP.

Then I headed back to the Palazzo, where I celebrated with a steak and a glass of red wine at the bar at Carnevino and then played in a $2/$4 cash game for a few hours and took a bunch of people's money. I drove home to Los Angeles the next day and didn't get off the couch for three days.

I took a week off from online poker after the WSOP to give my brain a chance to relax. I was seeing cards in my sleep. I started playing again and was right back into not just double duty but quadruple duty with poker and music. Everything was moving forward in Anthrax world. The songwriting for *Worship Music* was going really well, and there were big things on the horizon. We were on the verge of reuniting with Joey Belladonna and doing the first Big 4 shows with Metallica, Slayer, and Megadeth in Europe. I was also on tour with Pearl quite a bit at this point, which was really the best for me, getting to be the rhythm guitar player in my lady's band and watching her kick ass every night. Along with all this, The Damned Things record had come out and I was touring all over the planet with them as well. And all the while I was playing poker. If I wasn't on stage or sleeping, I was playing online. Looking back on it, I have no idea how I managed it all. I'd get asked in interviews all the time how I was able to do all these things, and I'd answer, "I had myself cloned."

This crazy amount of work not only continued all the way through 2010 and into 2011, but it got crazier. Pearl was pregnant, and that was the greatest news ever. I started coming home early from The Damned Things tours to spend more time at home with her. Meanwhile Anthrax was back in full-speed mode after a big US tour with Slayer and Megadeth in the fall of 2010, and there was no stopping that machine now that it was running again. Joey was back, and the Big 4 shows were happening, and all the struggles we were facing were yesterday's news. Pearl and I went to Las Vegas in January of 2011 and got married, surprising my father for his seventieth birthday celebration. We'd been talking about getting married for a while, and making it a part of my dad's birthday made it extra special. It was just a small group of family and friends, and the best Filipino Elvis impersonator ever married us.

Anthrax played the first US Big 4 show in April of 2011 at the Empire Polo Grounds outside of Los Angeles, and on the back of that triumph I had just renegotiated my deal with UB, signing a new two-year contract that was really too good to be true. The best job ever just kept getting better.

I'd been playing poker for just over three years, and it had become a huge part of my life. UB were very happy with what I brought to the company, and their ROI (return on investment) was working out very well for everyone involved. So 2011 was shaping up to be the best year of my life personally and professionally.

And then came Black Friday.

And we're right back where this tale started. The government takedown of online poker left a trail of destruction in its wake. Tens of thousands of people, players and industry folk alike, were suddenly out of jobs as a multi-billion-dollar industry vanished. Players couldn't get their money off the sites; I was hearing horror stories about players with their life savings gone, who had their money earmarked for college that they'd never be able to pay for now—story after terrible story. Nobody knew what was going on; it was chaos. Was the shutdown permanent? Could we play online in Europe from the United States? Would we ever get our money out? There were no answers. The people I knew who worked for UB were as much in the dark as I was and even worse off, because they had no jobs and had rent to pay and children to feed. I considered myself lucky. Even with my new deal at UB going up in smoke I had my awesome day job and had started pulling my money out of my online account months before Black Friday. I had always looked at my online poker account as a savings account. Whatever UB paid me and whatever I won online would just accumulate in my UB account. About six months before Black Friday I got a call from Will Griffiths, the guy who signed me up to play at UB and changed my life. Will was no longer at UB, but we had become friends and always stayed in touch. Will asked me if I had a lot of money online, and when I told him I did he said, "You should start taking it out." I asked him why and he told me, "The sites are having a really difficult time processing payments. There aren't any real processors anymore because of the UIGEA, and the sites have been at the mercy of shady companies that are ripping off the cash they are supposed to be paying out to players. It's costing the sites a lot of money, and I wouldn't be surprised if some of them stopped operating in the United States."

I told Will, "I haven't heard anything like this from the people at UB, and I haven't had any issues getting money off the site."

But he said, "Mate, just start taking it out."

So I did, and by the time Black Friday arrived I had most of my money off the site. I had told some of my player friends what I was doing, and they did the same. Still, no one saw Black Friday coming. I don't think anyone thought there would be a complete shutdown. If anything, most people I spoke to thought there would eventually be a deal made with the government to regulate and tax online poker. Why wouldn't there be a deal? There was so much money to be made by everyone. Since Black Friday there would have been potentially billions of dollars in tax money that could have gone directly into US infrastructure. It makes no sense.

If there is a positive I can take from poker ending, it's that it did. Black Friday made me decide to stop playing. Without poker I had a lot more free time, and it happened at the perfect moment. Pearl gave birth to our son, Revel, in June. I wouldn't have been able to maintain the double-duty schedule I had been living for the past four years, and poker would've been the thing to suffer. I wouldn't have been putting in the hours because I would rather be with my wife and baby. Being a dad meant so much more than anything else in my life.

Six years have passed since Black Friday, and the disastrous fallout of that day is still being cleaned up. A lot of players got their money back initially—PokerStars being the biggest of the online sites had the cash to pay all their players back. PokerStars made a deal with the government to buy Full Tilt and paid all their non-US players back as well as paying a $547 million fine to the government for operating in the United States after the UIGEA was voted into law. Paying the fine enabled PokerStars to be able to operate in the United States again as online poker slowly becomes legal on a state-by-state basis.

UB players as well as players on other smaller sites weren't so lucky, as tens of millions of dollars of players' money disappeared into a morass of promises, lost paper trails, offshore accounts, and, ultimately, theft. As of this writing the US attorney for the Southern District of New York recently contacted UB players so they could begin the process of making a claim for the money they had in their accounts seized by the Department of Justice. Hopefully this will bring financial closure to the thousands of UB players who got screwed.

I've kept in touch with a lot of the people I became friends with through poker, and we usually see each other at charity poker events (I took second out of seventy players in a charity tourney last year, winning a gold pen and a seat in a WSOP tourney I couldn't play because I was on tour) or they come out to Anthrax shows, and it's always fun to reminisce about the good ol' days over too many drinks. Sometimes I get to play in home games locally, the coolest being invited by Phil Hellmuth to play in a game at Steve Martin's house. Yes, that Steve Martin. Phil called and asked, "Hey Scott, are you home, and would you want to come play cards at Steve Martin's house?"

There's a question I'd never been asked before. I immediately answered, "Oh hell yeah! Thanks, Phil!" Then I thought about it for a second and said, "Uh, I'm not sure if I can. You guys may be playing at stakes way above my pay grade."

Phil laughed and said, "We're playing $5/$10, nothing crazy. Steve doesn't want anyone losing too much money in his house. It'd make him uncomfortable." Phil gave me the address, and a few nights later I was knocking on Steve Martin's door. I was freaking out. I'd been a fan since his *Let's Get Small* album. I love Steve Martin.

Steve opens the door and says, "You must be Scott. How are you?" And we shook hands and my nerves went away because he was so cool and the perfect host. I was standing in his dining room with Phil, Wayne Gretzky, Janet Jones, Wayne's daughter Paulina, Steve's wife Anne, and Phil's friend Chamath, a billionaire. Yes, it was another one of those who-let-me-in-here moments. Steve explained what was going to happen: "Okay, here's what we're going to do. We're going to all have some soup, and then we'll go downstairs and play some cards. Then we'll come back up for dinner and then go back downstairs to play cards until we're done. Sound good?" Yes, Steve, it sounds good. We had soup (Steve had caterers cooking for us), then we went downstairs to his amazing card room. It was a fun game, everyone was super-cool, and there was a lot of shit-talking. Steve was exactly as I imagined he'd be— quietly funny. We played for about an hour, and then we had dinner and then right back to hold 'em. I slipped right back into my game and ended up winning $500. I didn't care about the money; I had just spent five hours playing cards with Steve Martin. Oh yeah, and Wayne Gretzky.

My relationship with poker these days is that of an admirer from afar. I don't get to play live poker because I don't have time. I'm not complaining at all—I love my life. Being a husband and a father and having a full-time gig in Anthrax is the best, but it just doesn't leave much room for anything else. That's why online poker was so perfect for me. All I needed was my laptop. Poker has made its way back legally in three states so far: Nevada, New Jersey, and Delaware. It's only a matter of time before it becomes legal in most of the United States, and then watch out! Your boy will be back, playing the seniors tournament at the WSOP!

The good ol' days. Courtesy Scott Ian.

THE CONVERSATION

INT. BEDROOM—NIGHT

The telephone rings in Scott Ian's bedroom in the East Village apartment he is sharing with then Anthrax singer John Bush.

SCOTT: Hello?
DARRELL: Baldini!

Years before Darrell was riding on his tour bus up Third Avenue in Manhattan and passed a men's clothing store called Dino Baldinini. Darrell shortened it to Baldini, and it became Darrell's nickname for Scott.

Illustration by Stephen Thompson.

SCOTT: Hey Dime! What's going on, man?
DARRELL: Did I wake ya?

SCOTT: No, I'm actually just going to bed. It's all good, man. What's up?

DARRELL: I got that tape you sent of the record. You got some killin' motherfuckin' tunes on this album. Man, I'm catchin' a nut! I got the whole crew over here at the house, and we've been crankin' it over and over again. Record sounds great! Songs are great! Fuckin' killer, man. I fuckin' love it! Hope I get to jam some of this shit live with you motherfuckers when you come down here. Just wanted to tell you thanks so much for havin' me.

Darrell played on the songs "King Size" and "Riding Shotgun" on Anthrax's new album Stomp 442.

SCOTT: Thank you! Thank you for playing on the record. We fucking love jamming with you, you know that. You can come up and jam any time, brother.

Scott and Darrell start shootin' the shit, having a conversation. The whole time they are talking there's somebody screaming in the background. Screaming very loud in a high-pitched, pissed-off way, and not the kind of celebratory shouting there would normally be at a party.

YELLING GUY: NOBODY GIVES A FUCK ABOUT ME! NOBODY CARES ABOUT ME ANYMORE! In 1988 I was NUMBER ONE! Now no one cares. People only want to listen to bands like Pantera and Slayer and Anthrax. NOBODY CARES ABOUT ME ANYMORE!

The yelling goes on and on, and it is distracting Scott.

SCOTT: Darrell, Darrell, excuse me, but who the fuck is that? Who is that yelling in your house?

DARRELL: Aw, man. That's your boy "Sebastian Bach." Yeah, uhh, me and the crew we all went down to see him play tonight here in Dallas. He was at some club, and he fuckin' banged out a whole bunch of old Skid Row shit. We were all rockin' out and shootin' Blacktooths and I invited everyone back over to the house for a party afterward. His whole band and all the crew, and we were all havin' a hell of a good time . . .

Darrell's voice gets lower, almost to a whisper.

DARRELL, *cont*.: But your boy did a whole bunch of cocaine and basically just pissed everyone the fuck off with this fuckin' trip that he's been on, and everyone fuckin' split. Now it's just me and him left, and I can't leave my own house!

SCOTT: Oh, shit. That's not cool.

Scott hears "Sebastian" yelling in the background, just going on and on with all this "Nobody cares about me" bullshit.

SCOTT, *cont*.: Well, that sucks, man. What a fuckin' bummer. Can't you just call a taxi and he'll have to go back to his hotel?

DARRELL: I called him a taxi! He wouldn't get in it!

SCOTT: Fuck, man, what a bummer.

DARRELL: You know me. I'll fuckin' party all night long, whatever, all day, I don't give a fuck. Last man standing. But man, your boy's just gettin' on my fuckin' nerves. I just can't fuckin' deal with motherfuckers talkin' about old bullshit. Nobody cares about him, sayin' he wants to kill himself . . .

Scott is very concerned by this last statement.

SCOTT: He said he wants to kill himself?

DARRELL: Yeah! Motherfucker said, "If I ain't got my music, then what's life worth livin' for? I should just end it right now and kill myself."

SCOTT: Shit, what did you say?

DARRELL: I fuckin' told him, "Don't be fuckin' stupid, motherfucker! People love you, motherfucker!" I talked a whole bunch of happy shit, tryin' to cheer him up. But he just doesn't wanna hear it. He's too fuckin' high.

SCOTT: Man, this whole scenario is just . . .

Before Scott can finish his sentence Darrell starts shouting at "Sebastian."

DARRELL: GET OFF THAT, MOTHERFUCKER! WHAT'D I TELL YOU?

The call disconnects, and all Scott hears is a dial tone droning in his ear. There was a loud crash before the call went dead, and Darrell was yelling at "Sebastian." Scott is concerned for both his friends— Darrell because he's stuck in this shitty situation, and "Sebastian" because it sounds to Scott like he's so down on himself. It's now 3:30 a.m., and Scott, exhausted from a long day, decides he's going to bed. Scott figures it'll play itself out eventually and he'll talk to Darrell the following day to see what happened. Scott falls asleep almost immediately.

About thirty minutes later the phone rings again, waking Scott up, and he very groggily answers it.

SCOTT: Hello?

DARRELL: Baldini!

SCOTT: Hey Dime ...

DARRELL: Did I wake ya?

SCOTT: Yeah, uh, yeah ...

Scott slowly starts to wake up.

SCOTT, *cont.*: Yeah, it's fine, dude. What happened? I heard a big noise, you were yelling about something. What's going on? Did he leave?

DARRELL: Naw, motherfucker's still here.

SCOTT: All right, well, what happened?

DARRELL: That crash you heard was that motherfucker breaking my Kiss pinball machine! Took his fuckin' beer bottle and hurled it right through the fuckin' glass.

Illustration by Stephen Thompson.

SCOTT: WHAT? Oh man, what the fuck? You didn't throw him out of your house right after that?

DARRELL: What am I fuckin' supposed to do? Fight that motherfucker? I can't do that.

SCOTT: I don't know what to say ... man. The Kiss machine? That's fucking all kinds of fucked up.

DARRELL: Yeah, and he didn't just do that! He kicked over the smoke machine in my living room so the whole house is filled with smoke now. And now he's in my fuckin' backyard, and "Sebastian Bach" is chasin' the fuckin' goat around the swimming pool!

Illustration by Stephen Thompson.

Darrell has a goat with a pink goatee just like his. Scott starts laughing at the idea of "Sebastian" chasing a goat around the swimming pool. He has never heard that sentence before nor does he think anyone in the history of the English language, or any language, has said, "'Sebastian Bach' is chasin' the fuckin' goat around the swimming pool." Scott is laughing his ass off.

DARRELL: It ain't funny, motherfucker! This ain't funny!

SCOTT: *(Still laughing)* It's a lot funny, Darrell.

DARRELL: IT AIN'T FUNNY! You think if my fuckin' goat falls in the swimming pool, you think your fuckin' boy "Sebastian's" goin' in there with his white fuckin' boots on? FUCK NO! I'm goin' in there! I gotta get the fuckin' goat out!

Illustration by Stephen Thompson.

Scott is thinking of Darrell trying to wrestle a goat out of a pool. How would you even get a goat out of a fuckin' pool? Scott starts laughing even harder.

DARRELL: Don't laugh, motherfucker! That thing kicks me in the head, then what?

SCOTT: *(Calming down.)* I'm sorry. I apologize. I'm tired and a little bit delirious, and it's making me laugh.

DARRELL: It ain't funny man. I don't know what to fuckin' do. I just—I don't know what to do about this shit. I'm fuckin' over it. The guy's on my last fuckin' nerve. I can't handle it.

SCOTT: Hey, hey, HEY! I have an idea.

DARRELL: Yeah Baldini, what is it?

Scott, thinking about all the parties and all the shenanigans that go on at Darrell's house on a regular basis . . .

SCOTT: You get a lot of complaints, right? From your neighbors? You make a lot of noise in your house, you must.

DARRELL: Yeah, my neighbors hate me. Call the cops all the time. Where you going with this, Baldini?

SCOTT: What if I called the cops and said my neighbors were making too much noise and I give them your address? Then they'll send the cops over and "Sebastian" will have to leave. Problem solved.

Darrell doesn't answer right away, takes a beat, takes another, and then quietly and very seriously answers.

DARRELL: Baldini, that's a good idea, BUT you can't just call the cops on my house, like, planned and shit. It don't sit right with me, like, planning it like that. If the cops come, the cops come. If my real neighbors call the cops, they call the cops. But we can't do that. It sets a bad precedent.

SCOTT: Are there drugs, like, out on the table?

DARRELL: No! Your boy did all the drugs! There's no fuckin' drugs left.

Scott is disappointed that Darrell didn't like the idea and tries to sell it again.

SCOTT: Well, man, I don't know what to tell you. I really think I could . . .

And again before Scott can finish his sentence Darrell starts shouting at "Sebastian."

DARRELL: HEY MOTHERFUCKER, I SAID DON'T TOUCH THAT! GET . . .

The call disconnects again. Scott is at a loss now. Darrell's fucked, but what can he do? He tried to help, but Darrell shot it down. Scott is in New York, Darrell is in Fort Worth, Texas, and Scott doesn't know how to help his friend. It's almost four-thirty in the morning now, and Scott has to go to bed. Scott and John (who is fast asleep in the other bedroom) have shit to do the next day, so Scott goes back to sleep. About thirty minutes later the phone rings again.

SCOTT: *(sleepily)* Hello?

DARRELL: *(whispers)* Baldini.

SCOTT: Dime?

DARRELL: *(whispers)* Yeah.

SCOTT: What's wrong?

DARRELL: *(whispers)* I'm hiding in the closet.

SCOTT: *(incredulous)* You're hiding in the closet?

Illustration by Stephen Thompson.

DARRELL: *(hisses)* Quiet down, motherfucker—he'll hear you!

SCOTT: (whispers) You're hiding in the closet?

DARRELL: (quietly) I'm hiding in the closet. Motherfucker was in the kitchen, so I ran upstairs. I got a big ol' closet. I fuckin' ran in and pulled all my clothes down off the hangers on top of me so I just look like a pile of dirty laundry on the floor.

SCOTT: This is your plan? *This* is your plan? You're gonna fuckin'—

(Scott looks at the clock in his bedroom.)

—you've got at least two hours till the sun comes up. This is your plan?

DARRELL: (whispering loudly) What do you mean till the sun comes up? You think just 'cause the sun comes out, he's gonna leave. Like a vampire or some shit? Like, "Sun's up—gotta go!" That motherfucker's high as a kite. He might be here all day. I'm just gonna hang here, man. I'm fuckin' comfortable.

SCOTT: I don't know man. Just let me call the cops. It'll be over in fuckin' fifteen minutes. You'll be done, and go to bed.

DARRELL: Baldini, don't call the cops. No police. No police, I told you.

SCOTT: All right, man, okay. I don't know what to tell you.

DARRELL: Look, I'm fuckin' comfortable. I got a pair of pants rolled up under my neck for a pillow. I'm all good.

SCOTT: A pair of pants rolled up for a pillow. That's some plan. Look, I gotta go to bed. Just call me tomorrow and let me know what happened . . .

Scott hears the sound of the closet door crashing open.

KRRAK!!!

"SEBASTIAN": THERE YOU ARE, MOTHERTRUCKER! AAAAA-AARRRRRRGGGGGGHHHHH!

SMASH! KRAKK! WHAM! BASHH!

Scott hears what sounds like a tornado crashing through a house and "Sebastian" yelling at Darrell right before the call disconnects. Scott drops the phone; it sounded like "Sebastian" was physically coming through the phone line. Scott is really nervous now: he is friends with "Sebastian" and Darrell and is worried about their safety. It's taken a dark turn. Scott thinks it sounds like "Sebastian" is a bit depressed about his life, is having a crisis of confidence, thinks everybody can't fuckin' stand him, and is now hanging out with Scott's bro Darrell, who would rather hide in a closet than spend one more fuckin' second with him.

Scott thinks, What if this gets physical? What if they get in a fight or something? Or even worse? What if something crazy violent happens? Scott has read a lot of crazy things in the newspapers over the years about friends getting into altercations when booze/drugs are involved, and it's five in the morning and, Scott being a bit delirious, he decides to call the police. He feels he has to do it. If something were to happen to one of them, he'd never forgive himself for not doing something. So Scott, against Darrell's wishes, calls the cops.

911 OPERATOR: 911 emergency, hello?

SCOTT: Yes, I need to make a noise complaint.

911 OPERATOR: Yes sir, what's the address?

SCOTT: Yeah, my neighbors have been making a lot of noise. Here's the address . . .

Scott gives the 911 operator Darrell's address.

911 OPERATOR: Sir, are you okay?

SCOTT: Yeah, I'm fine. I just can't sleep. My neighbor's having a party, and there's a lot of screaming going on over there. I just can't sleep. Maybe you could send the police around.

911 OPERATOR: Sir, you're saying your neighbors in Fort Worth, Texas, are making too much noise and are keeping you awake,

but you're in an apartment in Manhattan. If this is some kind
of prank call, you should know we trace these calls and can
press felony charges against you . . .

Before the 911 operator can finish, Scott hangs up the phone like
it was on fire. Scott realizes the huge mistake he just made by
making what turns out to be a prank call to 911. Inadvertently or
not, they will arrest you for doing that. They know exactly where
you're calling from, they send the police, and they take you to jail.
All these thoughts are racing through Scott's brain as he tries to
make sense of this mess going on at five o'clock in the morning. He
knows he needs to get out of the apartment before the police arrive.
He decides to get dressed and head over to the twenty-four-hour
restaurant next door where he can watch for the police to arrive
and then, after they leave, go back to bed. As Scott is quickly getting
dressed he realizes that John Bush is sleeping and has no idea about
anything that's been going on. The police will ring the bell, and John
will buzz them into the building, and when he answers the door
they'll possibly end up arresting him. Scott finishes getting dressed
and is about to go wake up John to explain what happened and get
him out of the apartment when the phone rings.

Illustration by Stephen Thompson.

SCOTT: *(exasperated)* Hello?

DARRELL: Baldini!

SCOTT: Dime! WHAT THE HELL HAPPENED?

DARRELL: What the fuck are you all riled up about?

SCOTT: Dude, I don't have time for this anymore! The fucking cops are coming!

DARRELL: Whadda' you mean, the cops are coming, Baldini?

SCOTT: The cops are coming! They're coming to get me!

DARRELL: Why are the cops coming to get you?

SCOTT: *(very exasperated)* I called the cops to come to your house, but I gave them the Texas address, and I'm in New York City, so they think I made a prank call! Look, I have to go.

DARRELL: *(very serious)* Baldini, I fuckin' told you: DON'T. CALL. THE. COPS! You see what happens? You call the police, only bad shit happens! I told you it'd set a bad precedent! You're gettin' arrested now—God dammit . . .

SCOTT: Dime, I can't talk about it right now, I gotta go. I gotta wake up John Bush . . .

DARRELL: You gotta wake up John Bush? Why you gotta wake him up?

SCOTT: I can't leave him here for the cops to arrest him! Listen I HAVE TO GO. What happened before with "Sebastian" and the closet?

DARRELL: Aw man, your boy was pissed off when he found me in the closet. He was fuckin' mad. But I fuckin' talked a bunch of crazy shit at him, and he forgot and is listening to KISS downstairs right now.

SCOTT: Okay, good. I gotta go. I gotta go. I'll talk to you later.

DARRELL: All right, motherfucker. Call me back when you get out of jail! Ah ha ha ha ha ha!

Illustration by Stephen Thompson.

They both hang up. Scott rushes out of his bedroom and is just about to knock on John's door when the phone rings again. Before Scott can even say hello Darrell yells.

INT. LIVING ROOM, EARLY MORNING

DARRELL: Baldini!

SCOTT: Dude, I can't, I'm fuckin'—I gotta go!

DARRELL: Hold on! Someone wants to talk to you!

SCOTT: What are you talking about?

Scott hears Darrell handing the phone over to "Sebastian."

SCOTT, *cont.*: No, Dime! Not now! I have to . . .

"Sebastian" cuts Scott off midsentence, yelling.

"SEBASTIAN": *(excited)* Hey, mothertrucking Scott Ian! How you doing?

("Mothertrucking" was "Sebastian's" play on "motherfucking.")

SCOTT: "Sebastian," I can't talk to you. The cops are coming to my
house! I gotta go!

"SEBASTIAN": What? The cops are coming?

SCOTT: I gotta go! I can't fucking explain right now! Ask Darrell—
he'll tell you. I gotta go.

"SEBASTIAN": *(pissed off)* Oh, you're going to blow me off too?
You're going to be a dick? Yeah, you're in a fucking band people like. Nobody fucking likes my band!

SCOTT: *(exasperated)* "Sebastian," I love you, but I have to go!

"SEBASTIAN": *(yelling)* Hey man, that is fucking bullshit! Nobody
cares about me anymore! You know, I fucking wrote "I Remember You," and nobody remembers me!

SCOTT: "Bas," I'm sorry, I can't. I'm sorry. I gotta go. Good-bye.

Scott goes to hang up the phone.

"SEBASTIAN": Dude! Hold on! Somebody wants to say hello.

*Scott pauses, confused by the idea that there's someone else there,
and then this other voice gets on the phone.*

DAVE WILLIAMS: Hey Scott! How's it going? It's Dave Williams
from the band Drowning Pool.

*Scott knows Dave and, for a moment, is stopped dead in his tracks
by this new wrinkle, forgetting about the cops and everything else
going on.*

SCOTT: *(confused)* Uh, hey Dave. You've been there the whole time?

DAVE WILLIAMS: Yeah, sure have.

SCOTT: Huh, well, that's weird 'cause I just thought it was Darrell and "Sebastian" and the goat. I'm just confused. I didn't know someone else was there the whole time, and . . . anyway, I gotta go . . .

Scott starts to come back to reality.

SCOTT, *cont.*: The cops are coming to get me. I gotta get out of my house.

DAVE WILLIAMS: Yeah, Darrell told me. You shouldn't have called the cops, Baldini.

SCOTT: *(annoyed)* Yeah, great. Thanks, I know. Look, I gotta go. Sorry, Dave, I'm not blowing you off, but I really do gotta get out of here.

DAVE WILLIAMS: Hold on. Someone wants to say hi.

Scott hears "Sebastian" immediately back on the phone.

"SEBASTIAN": Hey mothertrucker! It's "Sebastian Bach" from Skid Row!

SCOTT: "Sebastian"? Yeah, I know . . .

And then the voice immediately changes back to Dave Williams's voice.

DAVE WILLIAMS: Hey, Scott, it's Dave Williams from the band Drowning Pool.

SCOTT: Huh?

And then the voice changes back again to "Sebastian's."

"SEBASTIAN": Hey mothertrucker, it's "Sebastian Bach" from Skid Row!

The two voices keep alternating back and forth over and over, and that's when Scott realizes that Dave Williams from the band Drowning Pool does the best "Sebastian Bach" impersonation in the world. Scott drops the phone on the floor, just standing there in a total state of shock. Scott is trying to comprehend what just happened over the last few hours keeping him awake all night and causing the police to be on the way to arrest him. Scott gets pulled out of his reverie by a little tiny voice coming out of the earpiece of the phone's handset.

DARRELL: *(yelling)* AAAAAHHHHHH, BALDINI, I GOT YOU!

Scott slowly picks up the handset off the floor.

SCOTT: *(quietly)* Darrell.
DARRELL: *(very happy)* BALDINI! HAHAHAHAHA! I GOT YOU, MOTHERFUCKER! YEAHHHH! You know what we did today?
SCOTT: *(quietly)* What'd you do, Dime?
DARRELL: Oh man, hahaha! Dave came over to the house around noon, we fired up the barbecue, cracked a couple of beers, and I said, "Hey motherfucker, you still do that "Sebastian Bach" shit?" And Dave said, "I sure do, Dime." So I told him, "Here's what we're gonna do tonight. We're gonna call motherfuckin' Baldini in New York City and are gonna keep that fucker up all night long makin' him think "Sebastian Bach's" gonna kill himself in my living room!"

Scott's mind is blown. This was all some incredible wind-up that Darrell had actually planned! Scott, still in shock and trying to make sense of it all, finally replies to Darrell.

SCOTT: Dime, you fuckin' got me. This was . . . it was amazing. I
don't know what to say. Congratulations, that was an awesome
fucking joke. I can't believe it. "Sebastian" was never there.
Wow.

DARRELL: Yeah, Baldini, I gotcha good. All right, I'll let you go to
sleep—oh, wait a minute, the cops are comin'. I told you not to
call the cops, Baldini! Ha ha ha! Have fun in jail. Bye!

*Scott stands in the living room, arms hanging at his sides, phone
dangling from his hand, shaking his head, and smiling.* Let the
cops come, *he thinks,* who cares. *He slowly hangs up the phone and
walks back into his bedroom, gets back into bed, and drifts off to
sleep.*

Epilogue, AKA REVENGE!

I talked to Darrell later that day. I didn't wake up until three in the
afternoon, and I remembered everything. Darrell called to see if I
went to jail, and I told him the cops never showed up—apparently
911 is a joke, just like Flavor Flav said. He was happy I didn't get
arrested and how that whole "'Don't call the cops, Baldini" was an
added bonus to the wind-up. We talked for a bit about how amazing Dave Williams's impression of "Sebastian" was, and at the end
of the call Darrell said, "All right, see ya, Baldini, and don't forget:
'Sebastian Bach,' motherfucker!" and hung up.

I was naïve to think I'd heard the last of this.

For three years after that—for THREE YEARS—especially on
the tour we did in 1997–1998, anytime I saw Darrell he'd bring
it up. I'd be on his bus late at night driving to the next city, and
we'd be watching KISS from the Cow Palace in 1975 on video, and
he'd turn around and look at me and say, "Ain't this fuckin' cool?"

And before I could answer he'd quietly mutter, "Sebastian Bach, motherfucker" and then get right back into the KISS video. He'd zing me with that all the time. I would be eating lunch, and he'd walk by with a big smile and ask how the catering was and then as he was walking away he'd look back and growl, "Sebastian Bach, motherfucker." He'd randomly call and leave me a voicemail just saying, "Sebastian Bach, motherfucker." He held that sword over my head for three years, and I didn't know how to get him back. And I had to, because if you don't come back at him, he'll lose some respect for you. It's part of the game. He takes it just as hard as he can give it.

So it's toward the end of 1998 and I'm in Orlando, Florida, with Anthrax on tour. This is three years after The Conversation. I'm at dinner with Don Bernstine, the head of acquisitions for the Hard Rock. He was the guy who'd travel around the world to buy guitars for the Hard Rock to hang in their restaurants, casinos, and so on. Don was a great dude, a real friend. He was also friends with Darrell. I tell Don the whole story about The Conversation, and the first thing he asks is, "Well, what did you do to get him back?"

I say, "Nothing, man. I haven't thought of anything, and I've been trying. How do you fuck the unfuckable? I can't figure it out."

And Don says, "Well, man, I have an idea. Do you want to get him back right now? I know that motherfucker inside out. We could get him back right now if you want."

I said, "I'd be well into that."

He says, "All right, follow my lead."

Don takes out his phone, puts it on speakerphone, and calls Darrell's house. Darrell's wife, Rita, answers the phone.

RITA: Hey Bernstine.

DON: Hey Rita. Is Darrell there?

RITA: No, he's at rehearsal.

DON: I just wanted to let you guys know that our vault in Orlando was broken into.

This was a true story. A couple of weeks before this night the Hard Rock vault was broken into, and a whole bunch of guitars were stolen. Orlando is where the Hard Rock's headquarters are, and the vault is where they keep the super-rare guitars, clothing, and memorabilia until it goes out and gets hung up in one of their properties. I got to go there once and actually got to wear Gene Simmons's full-on Love Gun tour costume. It was big on me, but it was very cool to wear it.

RITA: Yeah, I heard about that. That's fucked up, Bernstine.

DON: Well, I just wanted you guys to know we've been doing an inventory, and Darrell's Crown Royal guitar is one of the guitars that was stolen. I just wanted you to hear it from me and to help get the word out there that it's been ripped off.

This was not a true story.

Illustration by Stephen Thompson.

The Crown Royal guitar was a one-of-a-kind Dimebag Darrell Washburn signature model. It was painted in what Darrell called "Clown Royal purple," and it came in a custom case in which they cut out a section of the hard foam in the inside of the case into the shape of a Crown Royal bottle so you could actually carry a bottle of whiskey in the guitar case in case of an emergency. There were times when they would run out of Crown on the bus, and Darrell would tell the driver to pull over so he could get the emergency bottle out of the guitar case. Don had purchased this guitar from Darrell, and it was safe and sound, hanging on a wall in a Hard Rock somewhere.

But Darrell didn't know that.

RITA: Oh that sucks, man. Well, I'll tell Darrell. I'm sure he'll call you soon.

About twenty minutes later Don's phone rings, and it's Darrell. Don puts it on speakerphone.

DARRELL: Hey Bernstine. Rita told me what happened. I'm really sorry about that. It fuckin' sucks, man. You guys paid me a lot of money for that shit. It's never gonna get to hang up somewhere. People won't get to enjoy it. That's just a fuckin' bummer, man. If there's anything I can do to help you . . .

DON: Well, actually, Darrell, there is something you can do. I've got kind of a weird situation here.

DARRELL: What's that, Bernstine?

DON: Well, Anthrax is in town, and I got a call from Scott Ian this afternoon. He said he's at a pawnshop in downtown Orlando, and he thinks the Crown Royal guitar is at this pawnshop.

DARRELL: Really! Well, tell the motherfucker to just get the guitar and bring it back to you—problem solved.

DON: Well, you see, this is the problem. Scott called me to verify if this guitar could possibly be hanging in a pawnshop, and I said, "You know, Scott, it might be there because we had a break-in." So, Dime, it seems like someone didn't know they had such a rare guitar, and now it's hanging in a pawnshop. Scott told me they only wanted three hundred dollars for it.

DARRELL: Three hundred dollars?

DON: Yes, and Scott bought it. He bought your guitar.

Illustration by Stephen Thompson.

DARRELL: Hold on, Bernstine. You're tellin' me Baldini got the Crown Royal guitar for three hundred dollars?

DON: Yes, that's what I'm telling you.

DARRELL: Okay, so what's the problem then? Is he just gonna bring it down to your office? What's the problem? He brings the guitar back, and you pay that motherfucker three hundred dollars—whatever, I'll pay you back. I'll give you the three hundred bucks, or tell him I'll give him three hundred dollars, whatever it is, problem solved, you get the guitar back.

DON: Well, Dime, I wish it was that simple. Here's the story. We've been doing inventory at the vault and trying to figure out where all the guitars are and what's missing and what isn't missing. And the Hard Rock is being investigated by forensic accountants, and we've got insurance adjusters here, and it's just been crazy, and they're up our ass about everything . . .

So Don tells Darrell a tale about the break-in and what he is supposedly dealing with. He weaves a black widow's web of deceit to fool Darrell. It has to be bulletproof to get one over on Dime, and this web of bullshit is all based in the truth of how the vault was broken into. It's good. Really good. So Don tells Darrell about how accountants, insurance agents, and the police are investigating all the employees who have access to the vault and that they have concluded that it must be an inside job, that the people who work at the Hard Rock are stealing the guitars themselves and selling them.

DON: Darrell, remember when I sent you those change-of-ownership papers for the guitar a few months ago?
DARRELL: Yeah.
DON: Well, you never signed those papers and sent them back to me, did you?
DARRELL: Uhh, no Bernstine, I didn't.
DON: Well, because of that, the Hard Rock never officially owned the Crown Royal guitar, and yet it was here and now it's missing and I'm getting the blame for it. They think I stole it, that somehow I cooked the books, and now I'm in jeopardy of losing my job. I could end up going to jail, AND the Hard Rock is in jeopardy of losing their whole

insurance policy on all their guitars because of insurance fraud, and it'll cost them millions of dollars to get a new one. So I need to get the guitar back from Scott.

While Don is telling Darrell this brilliant gem of a lie, I am calmly taking it all in, intently paying attention, drinking it all in like a fine whiskey, waiting for my turn to retaliate. I also really was drinking a fine whiskey.

DARRELL: Yeah, so what's the problem? Give him three hundred dollars and get the guitar back.

And then Don drops the bomb.

DON: Scott wants fifteen thousand dollars for the guitar.

I have to cover my mouth to stop from spraying whiskey all over Don from across the table.

DARRELL: HE WHAT?
DON: Scott wants fifteen thousand dollars for the guitar. He knows how much we pay for these things, and I guess he sees the chance to make some money and, you know, whatever, I can't blame the guy—he's got us over a barrel. He wants to make a little cash.
DARRELL: A LITTLE CASH?! Hold on, Bernstine! That motherfucker's your friend and he's my friend, and he's tryin' to fuckin' work you for fifteen thousand dollars? FUCK THAT SHIT! Goddamn Baldini, what the fuck?! Why don't you just call the cops, motherfucker? They'll get the guitar back for you.

Darrell brings up the police, and I have an idea. I quickly write a note on a napkin for Don: *NO COPS! Just like in Darrell's call to me. No cops.* You have to love when things come full circle.

DON: No cops, Darrell. I can't call the police because then they will take the guitar and it will go into evidence, and I'm still the one who's going to get the blame. I'm the one who's going to get fucked in this scenario because I paid you for the guitar, and I never got that change-of-ownership signed. I've already talked to my boss—they're gonna write the check to Scott just to avoid all the fucking issues wrapped up in this mess, mainly because the Hard Rock can't afford to lose its insurance policy.

Don is good. He's killing it. I high-five him and walk over to the bar for another round of drinks.

DARRELL: Fuck that shit, Bernstine! I'm callin' Baldini right now! Talk some sense into that motherfucker.

Illustration by Stephen Thompson.

DON: Well, that's why I was calling you, Darrell. Maybe if
  Scott hears your voice and how upset you are, he'll change
  his mind about wanting fifteen grand.
DARRELL: Goddamn right. I'll call that motherfucker right
  now! Good-bye.

My phone immediately starts ringing, and I let it go to voicemail. Don and I listen to the message: "Baldini, it's Dime. Hey man,
call me back. I need to talk to you right away." While we're listening to the message and for the next five minutes he calls back over
and over and over, each message getting angrier and angrier. Don
and I stop laughing long enough to finish our drinks and order another round. Don picks up his phone to call Darrell back, and I ask
him what's next, and he smiles and says, "Oh watch this."

DON: Hi Darrell, did you get a hold of Scott?
DARRELL: Naw, man. I can't get him on the phone. It just keeps
  going to voicemail!
DON: Okay, okay, well, Scott called me about five minutes
  ago—let me ask you a question, Darrell: Did you ever tell
  Scott how much we paid you for the Crown Royal guitar?
DARRELL: No, why would I? It's none of his business.
DON: Well, Scott knows we paid you $15,000, and now he
  wants $20,000. He figures it's worth more now.
DARRELL: WHAT THE FUCK, BERNSTINE? You tell that
  Baldini motherfucker he's not getting a fuckin' dime!
  FUCK THIS SHIT! This is a bunch of goddamn bullshit
  if I ever heard some!
DON: Darrell, Darrell, hold on, let me . . .
DARRELL: No, you hold on, Bernstine. I ain't done talking yet!
  I am tellin' you right now, Bernstine, if you guys pay him

for that guitar, I will NEVER speak to you again. And you tell Baldini when you see him that when I see him next month, I'll fuckin' take care of him!

Illustration by Stephen Thompson.

Darrell hangs up the phone. Don and I do a triple high-five across the table. It's going better than I could've imagined. I am reveling in the moment, and I tell Don, "Dude, do you think we could keep this going for a year? Play a really long game? Get actors involved as cops, and so on?" I was thinking really big.

Don laughs, takes a drink, and says, "Scott, I appreciate how evil you are, and how evil I am, and your need for revenge, but let me ask you something: Were you ever angry at Darrell about the 'Sebastian' call?"

I said, "Fuck no. Maybe I was a little angry at the fake-'Sebastian' they created, but that person didn't really exist, so how could I be angry with him? No, I loved it. That prank call was fucking amazing."

Don nods and smiles like a wizened old wizard and says, "Exactly. You heard Darrell—he is actually angry. Have you ever known Darrell to be angry?"

I thought about it for a minute and said, "No. Never. I've known that dude, like, twelve years now, and I didn't even know he could get angry."

Don said, "Right? He's always just Darrell. We really got under his skin with this idea of you making a pile of cash off his guitar and my vulnerable position."

"Yeah, you're right," I replied. "I hear what you're saying. I don't want him to think I'm 'Baldini motherfucker.' I don't want to be that guy to him. All right, we'll call him back. Let's end it. Let's figure it out. We'll order another drink, and then we'll call him back."

Don says, "What do we want to do? How are we getting out of this?"

I said, "Follow my lead," and we put our two big noses together and conferred.

Don calls Darrell back. Darrell answers the phone, and before Don can even get a word out Darrell says,

DARRELL: I told you, Bernstine, if you're paying Baldini, we're fuckin' done. Good-bye.

DON: DON'T HANG UP! Darrell, please don't hang up. I've got somebody in my office here. I've got some news—I think we've got this shit figured out. I just didn't want to put him right on the phone with you. I wanted to make sure it was okay with you because . . .

DARRELL: I don't give a fuck, Bernstine! I've wasted enough time on this bullshit. Put him on the phone!

Bernstine hands me the phone and I yell, "SEBASTIAN BACH, MOTHERFUCKER!"

Illustration by Stephen Thompson.

There's a slight pause, and then Darrell says, "BALDINI! HA-HAHA, BALDINI! Motherfucker! You been there this whole—WOW, you got me back! 'Sebastian Bach,' motherfucker! Holy shit! You fuckin' got me back! It's been what, three years? You fuckin' had me goin'—the two of you motherfuckers! I never stood a chance! HAHAHAHA!"

I said, "Hey Dime, how are ya? HAHAHAHAHA!"

Darrell said, "Does it feel good, Baldini?"

I said, "Dude, it feels fuckin' great."

We were both laughing and Darrell says, "Goddammit, when you got on the phone and said, 'Sebastian Bach, motherfucker'—ya got me, Baldini! Trying to make a dime offa Dime! All right you two, have a drink on your old brother Dimebag, and I'll talk at ya later!" And then he made this bobcat scratching sound that he would always do (he would do a move with his hand at the same time, like a claw scratching at you) and hung up the phone.

I was basking in the afterglow of hilarious revenge and felt like Darrell was proud of me for coming back at him so strong. I couldn't have done it without Don, and we toasted to Darrell many more times that night.

And from 1998 until Darrell was taken from us at the end of 2004, he never said "Sebastian Bach, motherfucker" to me ever again.

RIP Dimebag Darrell Abbott

RIP Don Bernstine

I hope you two are getting your pull and having a blast!

BATHTUB PIKE

For all intents and purposes I shouldn't be the fan of seafood that I am.
Even against a myriad number of compelling reasons to avoid
the delicacies of the sea, I find myself having no problem eating a shrimp head or puffer fish or any other strange thing from
the sea that *extreme eater* Andrew Zimmern would eat (if I eat
tuna balls slathered in durian, do I get my own show too?). I'm a
Jew, and it's in my genetic makeup to hide, like a vampire from
the sun, from shellfish. And besides the religious thing, seafood can kill you. Shouldn't that be reason enough to not eat it?
How about the fact that if you saw something that looked like
a crab or lobster skittering across your kitchen floor when you
turned on the lights, you'd do nothing short of napalming the
monstrosity.

As a kid, my practicing Jewish friends would tell me horror
stories about an uncle who was paralyzed after eating a bad clam
or a neighbor who contracted gout from a bad piece of fish. And
I certainly didn't need my hypocritical shrimp-cocktail-eating-
at-Bar-Mitzvahs-friends to tell me about the dangers of oysters.
Those stories were real urban legends, tales of murdering mol-
lusks and brutal bivalves poisoning everyone in their wake.

We used to go to my grandfather's house for the Passover
holidays. Before my grandparents moved to Florida they lived
in Queens, and my memories of their house are of small, dark,
oppressive rooms and plastic slipcovers. My grandfather was a
strict Orthodox Jew, and Passover was a long, dark day of standing
and sitting and standing and sitting and lots of oldies speaking

Hebrew and my brother and I doing everything we could to sneak a piece of matzo without any of the Passover Nazis catching us.

On one of those long days we arrived at their house early so my parents could help out and my brother and I could suffer even longer than usual. We didn't even get the payoff of the hide the matzo game that all our friends got to play. If it wasn't in my grandfather's Seder book, it wasn't part of Passover, so there was no money exchanging hands. On that day we arrived early, and I was roaming around the upstairs of the house unattended, exploring the mysteries of these people from Poland and Russia. I walked into a bathroom and noticed that the tub was full of water. As I got closer to the full tub, my curiosity roused as to why the paint-chipped, drain-ringed bathtub was filled with water. I could imagine my grandfather saying, "Who ran the bath? Such a waste, all this water—someone take a bath already!"

This bath wasn't for me, though.

I looked over the edge of the tub and saw a fish lazily swimming around. Initially I froze, my eight-year-old brain filled with surprise and fear. I thought, *Did that fish somehow swim up the pipes from the sewers and get into Grandpa's tub?* I didn't know how NYC plumbing worked, so I checked the toilet. No fish in there, just the long weird fish lolling in my grandfather's bathtub.

I ran downstairs to ask about my grandparents' new pet. "Grandpa, grandpa, there's a fish in the bathtub!"

And then to my horror: "Of course there's a fish in the bathtub. It's the pike for the gefilte fish."

I can remember standing there confused at this statement. Pike for the gefilte fish? In your gross tub that all you dusty old people bathe in upstairs? And then I thought about all the previous times I ate gefilte fish in that house, and I think I swooned a bit. It was one of the seminal moments of my life.

Guess who didn't eat the gefilte fish that day or any other day ever again? It was hard enough watching everyone at the table shoveling it into their mouths and talking with mouthfuls of bathtub pike. I still gag just thinking about it.

You—or actually I—would think that a moment like that would put me off fish forever. Tub fish, yes, and as a kid I'd ask my parents where whatever fish they were asking me to eat came from. The East River, Lake Erie, the puddle underneath the overpass after it rains—no problem. Just no tub fish, thank you.

IN THE END . . .

. . . is a song on the Anthrax album *Worship Music*. It is *the* song, the centerpiece of the album, with all the other songs built on top of it. I wrote this piece about it back in 2012, a year after *Worship Music* came out. It's unusual for me to have written a tribute to a song we wrote—that's something I've never done before. This song just stayed with me in a different way after we were done recording and the album was released. It spoke to me, constantly pulling me, telling me that its story needed to be told.

"In the End" started out as something completely different back in 2007 when Charlie and I first started working on it, and it was an inauspicious beginning for a song if there ever was one. We were working on an idea, a strong if unfocused idea, and to make matters even more intangible, we had no idea who else would even be in the band this time around. At that point it was just the two of us.

The original version of the song is mostly unrecognizable now. Between its genesis in 2007 and finishing it in 2011 it went through revision after revision. We were never satisfied, always just missing the mark, but we stayed with it because we knew there was something there, something strong that kept us engaged even through all the frustrations we experienced while trying to find the song within our idea. Our usual MO of Charlie coming up with a catalyst riff to get us jamming and building an arrangement was not working. This song wasn't going to be like "Madhouse" or "I Am the Law" or "Only," songs that came together very quickly. This song was tough and refused to open up to us easily. Like some kind of difficult puzzle, it was making us solve its mysteries. We kept at it, every few weeks revisiting and tweaking until, by 2009, we had a "finished" version of the song that we titled "Down Goes the Sun." And still we knew it was not as good as it should've been and actually may not have even made the record.

This was the song that we wanted to write as a tribute to our late friends Dimebag Darrell and Ronnie James Dio. It would be our first chance to say how we felt about those guys in the context of what we do and how deeply they influenced us. The riffs were telling us to write about them, about our friends. Epic in scope with just the right balance of melancholy and aggression, it sounded like a proper tribute to two men who had meant so much to us.

Except it wasn't yet perfect and it had to be. It had to be perfect to honor them.

First and foremost Darrell was our friend. We'd been on this crazy path together since we met in 1986. His impact on our lives will never be forgotten and will always be missed. He played on three Anthrax records. That pretty much says it all. He was truly the sixth member of the band. Getcha' pull!

Ronnie, what can I say? I started out as a fan from his work with Rainbow and then of course followed him to Black Sabbath. I saw Ronnie for the first time on the Heaven & Hell tour in 1980. He was incredible, taking Sabbath to new heights with the power of his voice. On the Mob Rules tour my friend Jimmy (who knew Ronnie) was able to score us some passes. We knocked on Ronnie's hotel room door and Ronnie said, "Hey guys, I just got out of the shower. Here's your passes—see you after the show," and he slid the passes under the door to us. I couldn't believe it.

We met him after the amazing show. I had a brief chance to shake his hand and stammer a hello, or at least try to, as I was so sweaty and nervous. Cut to years later, and I'm meeting Ronnie again backstage at the 1987 Castle Donington Monsters of Rock festival. Eighty thousand people were there to see Cinderella, Wasp, Anthrax, Metallica, Dio, and Bon Jovi. I walked over to Ronnie, and before I finished introducing myself he told me we had met before and that he remembered meeting me backstage in New Jersey five years earlier. That's who he was. He would make an effort to put people at ease. He always had a kind word and a smile. He was a mentor to us in so many ways, mainly on how to be so fucking cool. Anthrax was supporting him on tour in 2004, and I remember standing on the side of the stage night after night, blown away by the power he possessed and also giving him Yankees' playoff game scores between songs. Yes, Ronnie was as fanatical about the Yankees as I am. To have had the privilege to become friends with one of my heroes was an incredible experience.

As 2009 became 2010 we were still trying to crack this song. And then Charlie found the bells. He added bells, playing a dark melody that he included in a new arrangement. Suddenly it was clear; the song had revealed itself—the bells had unlocked its secrets. We made a minor tweak in the chorus, combining Charlie's new idea with one of our previous ideas, and the song was done.

It was one of those moments of clarity when you just know something is perfect. The song was finally the song.

Now we needed words that could stand up to and elevate the power of the music.

I wasn't sure how to even try to express what I felt about my two friends. It was excruciating. Every lyric I came up with sounded cheesy to me. I finally had the music that lived up to the task of honoring our friends; now I needed the words to convey the emotions. I kept hitting a wall, and then Charlie sent me a line, "Lone star was dark tonight," and the wall in my mind crumbled and the words came pouring out, my emotions translating into lyrics that I felt did Darrell and Ronnie justice.

I'll leave the rest to you my friends. You can listen for yourselves. Enjoy it, and I hope it fucks your world the same way Darrell and Ronnie fucked with mine.

Illustration by Stephen Thompson.

YOUR HERO SHOULD NEVER WEAR DAISY DUKES

(Unless Your Hero Is Daisy Duke)

It was a hot Los Angeles day in the industrial wasteland of faceless, low, concrete buildings, chop shops, nameless bars, railroad tracks that go nowhere, and mysterious warehouses somewhere between North Hollywood and Burbank.

One of those days so hot that the tar is melting on the street and if I stepped on it, it'd eat the shoe right off my foot like a snake swallowing a large rat, slow and deliberate with purpose, my poor shoe sinking into the street, choking on the hot blacktop until it disappears and the street closes over it like it never happened. It was that fucking hot.

I was inside one of those mysterious warehouses filled with band rehearsal rooms that are gloriously temperature controlled to a balmy 68 degrees, rehearsing for an upcoming Anthrax tour.

After jamming for an hour it was time for a break. I took off my guitar and headed out to take a piss and grab a cup of coffee. I walked out of the rehearsal room, and before I could even close the door behind me a vision leaning over the Ms. Pac-Man machine stopped me dead in my tracks.

I was looking at the perfectly tanned back and legs of an almost naked person, except for a pair of the shortest short-short Daisy Dukes (shorts made famous by Catherine Bach on the awesome eighties TV show *The Dukes of Hazzard*), with perfectly tanned butt cheeks hanging out of them. I was horrified. I was horrified because this wasn't a beautiful California girl out of some perfect summertime Beach Boys–esque dream; it was a nightmare. It was stupefying. It was so fucked up that it was impossible to tear my gaze away from this unfathomable, disturbing sight.

It was my hero.

It was Lemmy.

I won't poison your eyes with a photo, you can Google the offending image if you dare. It's out there.

It was Lemmy standing there playing Ms. Pac-Man, all tanned and barefoot except for a pair of the shortest Daisy Dukes I had ever seen, a half-smoked cigarette burning away in an ashtray as he tried to avoid being eaten by Blinky, Pinky, Inky, and Clyde.

LEMMY.

My hero. The coolest, hardest, toughest, smartest, funniest guy in the history of rock and roll. I couldn't make sense of it, nor should I have been able to. The lack of context made the apparition deeply surreal. At that point I'd been a Motörhead fan for fourteen years. Fourteen years of Lemmy in head-to-toe denim and leather and then—BOOM. It was like seeing Clint Eastwood in a Speedo. It's just not right. It's not cool.

I forgot about going to the bathroom and getting a coffee and instead ducked right back into our room. I figured I'd wait a bit and then hopefully Lemmy would be gone. Twenty minutes later I peeked out the door and he was still there. I found out from a friend who worked at the rehearsal studio that Motörhead was also rehearsing there for the next week. Normally I would've been very excited about this, but having just witnessed what I saw I was calling everything I knew into question. Seeing your hero wearing Daisy Dukes can do that to you. My world was turning upside down. I just wanted to go back in time to when Lemmy wore black jeans and boots. I asked my friend if he too had seen what no one should ever see, and before he spoke I could see in his eyes that he had. I hugged him tight, commiserated, told him, "Everything is going to be okay," and headed back to the room to finish rehearsal, keeping the secret of what I had witnessed to myself so as to not freak out the rest of the band.

When I got to rehearsal the next day I snuck, Batman-like, to our practice room, hypervigilant so as to not have my eyes molested. As I turned a corner there he was again, leaning over Ms. Pac-Man, cigarette burning in an ashtray, naked except for the Daisy Dukes. I averted my eyes and just kept walking, and as I was about to walk into our room Lemmy quickly turns to me (still playing the game) and says, "Hi Scott, how are ya?"

Jarred by his sudden query and in no way ready to have a conversation with my pants-challenged hero I mumbled, "Hey Lem," and without stopping I opened the door to our room and was safe. Whew.

This went on for days.

I spent as much time as I could in our room, not wanting to bump into Lem, but it was useless. I'd invariably see him in the hall or playing the machine or out front having a smoke, face up to the sun, getting even more tan than he already was. I was avoiding him, and it was bumming me out because I really wanted to hang and didn't want him to think I was being a dick—which I was, because he'd say hello or try to start a conversation, and I'd have some bullshit excuse, so I decided I would get up the nerve to directly confront the issue at hand. I had to know why.

The next day I got to rehearsal, dropped my stuff off in the room, and headed straight to the lounge where Lemmy was in his usual spot playing Ms. Pac-Man, cigarette accompaniment, no wardrobe change. I took a deep breath and steeled myself, summoning the balls to question my hero's fashion choice. I sidled up next to the Ms. Pac-Man machine and said, "Hey Lem, how are ya?"

"Good, Scott. How are you?" he replied without looking away from the game.

"I'm okay, thanks. Um, uh, cough, um, hey Lem, mind if I ask you a question?"

He gave a barely perceptible nod and raised an eyebrow, staying focused on Ms. Pac-Man's health.

This was it, my moment of truth.

"Uh, what's with the shorts?"

As the last word fell out of my mouth it was like a chill came down over the room and everything got silent. Lemmy picked up his smoke and slowly turned his head toward me. It's like I had tunnel vision and could only see his mouth taking a long drag on his cigarette and then blowing the smoke into my face, the acrid cloud angrily surrounding my head as if to punish me for daring to question the man. As the smoke cleared I could see Lem staring at me, looking at me in slo-mo from head to toe and back up again, studying. Already nervous from having questioned my hero and now paranoid because he was eyeballing me so intently, I looked down at myself to see if there was something wrong, to see what he was seeing. Everything looked right to me: Vans slip-ons, camo shorts just past my knees, Maiden T-shirt—what I would deem proper summer attire for a guy like me. I immediately regretted the question and just wanted to get out of the conversation as I stood there nervously waiting for his reply. I looked up, and Lemmy, still laser focused on me with his best spaghetti western stare, points with his cigarette hand at my shorts and growls, "Scotty, those are pants"—and then pointing at his Daisy Dukes—"these are shorts."

And upon uttering that completely inarguable statement he immediately turned back around to the game that he had never

stopped playing with his other hand the whole time he was looking at me.

And Ms. Pac-Man was still alive.

What the hell?

So not only is he Lemmy, but he's the Fonz too?

What could I possibly have to say? He shut me down with
truth, and there was nothing I could do but accept his logic. It
didn't mean I had to like my hero wearing Daisy Dukes; it meant I
understood why and that made the next few days at the rehearsal
studio much more fun.

We finished up rehearsal and headed out on tour.

Over the next decade I crossed paths with Lem many times,
whether it was me going to a Motörhead show, Anthrax and
Motörhead playing festivals together, or Anthrax opening for
Motörhead on tour. I always had a great time hanging with him
and felt privileged that I could just sit and have a drink and con-
verse with him, usually about politics and war.

In 2009 I was asked if I would be interested in being inter-
viewed for a Lemmy documentary, and of course I answered yes.
During the interview I was asked whether I had any "crazy Lemmy
stories," and the Daisy Dukes tale immediately popped into my
head. I ended up telling an abbreviated version of this story for
the movie. Months later I heard from the director that the movie
was finished and my segment was getting a lot of laughs at screen-
ings. I was just happy to be a part of documenting my friend and
that people were getting my bit in the spirit of good humor for
which it was intended. Once the movie was out it seemed like everywhere I went people would come up to me and tell me how
much they loved the Daisy Dukes story. My visual nightmare
seemed to connect with people.

Anthrax were on the Mayhem festival in the summer of 2012
along with Slipknot, Slayer, and Motörhead. I hadn't seen Lemmy

since the release of the movie, and I was really excited to get to spend what was going to be like summer camp across the states with Lem and company. The first show of the tour was at the San Manuel Amphitheater, a big outdoor venue in San Bernardino, California. When I walked into the artist area backstage I saw Lemmy sitting outside his dressing room having a smoke. I walked over to say hi, even before heading to my dressing room to get rid of my bags, as I was excited to see my friend and catch up. Lemmy gave me the nod of recognition—slight head raise and an arched eyebrow as he took a drag on his cigarette.

"Hey Lem, how are ya?" I asked.

"Good, Scotty. How are you," he replied in that unmistakable growl of his.

"I'm good, man, thanks. Excited for the tour?"

"Yeah, yeah, should be good, ya know," he answered. Then he took another long pull on his smoke, exhaled staring at me, and said, "I hear you've been getting a lot of laughs in my movie with that story you tell about my shorts."

Awkward. Was Lemmy mad at me?

Suddenly I was twenty years old again, meeting him for the first time, all nervous and sweaty, my voice seemingly going up an octave, and I stammered, "Uh yeah, ha ha ha, yeah, that story. Ummm, it's funny, right?" No answer from Lemmy. He sat there silently, slowly smoking and looking off somewhere else. "So yeah, the, uh, the movie was really good, Lem. Congratulations on that," I stuttered, not being able to deal with the silence he was throwing my way.

His reply was another long, pregnant pause, and another cloud of Lemmy smoke exhaled in my direction. Finally, after what felt like forever, Lemmy, still staring at me, growls, "What the hell were you doing looking at my ass anyway?"

And with that microphone drop of a reply, Lemmy flicked his cigarette butt to the floor and crushed it with his boot, and as he walked into his dressing room he turned around toward me and smiled.

ACKNOWLEDGMENTS

Thank you to Pearl Aday, Jason Rosenfeld, Dominick DeLuca, Mark Osegueda, Steven Wiig, Kirk Hammett, Charlie Benante, Marc Paschke, Frank Bello, Lisa Tenner, and Erik Luftglass for helping with the when, where, and why of it all.

Thank you to my editor Ben Schafer for being awesome.

Thank you to Justin, Lissa, and everyone at Da Capo Press.

Thank you to Marc Gerald and Kim Koba at UTA.

Thank you to everyone who read *I'm the Man,* giving me the opportunity to write this one. Cheers my friends, these tales of mirth and mayhem are for you.

Thank you to everyone in this book that I have crossed paths with over the last forty years—here's to us; who is as good as us? Damn few, and they're all dead!